# Pride of the Wineries

# Pride of the Wineries

## The first region-by-region analysis and listing of California Wines.

### Edited by Harold I. Silverman

A California Living Book

# CONTENTS

## Pride of the Wineries

## The California Living Wine Collection

# Wine Publications

# Restaurants and Retail Stores

# Pride
# of the
# Wineries

# Foreword

It is most unusual when a single book combines the knowledge and talents of three outstanding authorities on a single multi-faceted subject, especially when the subject is California's winelands and its wines. This is such a book; researched, written, and packed with the knowledge, experience, and wisdom of noted authorities Bob Thompson, Harvey Steiman, and Mildred Howie, each noted for command of the subject and for the ability to explain each aspect of wine clearly and entertainingly.

— Leon D. Adams

# Editor's Note

With a dose of pleasure — and a dash of irony — we explain the genesis of the underlying approach of this book and its title.

First, the approach — which explains why we're so pleased by the flattering words of Leon Adams on page two. Even he, the sometimes feisty, always meticulous dean of American wine writers, has forgotten that his son Gerald was the first to run our theory by the senior Adams — the idea of assessing and comparing California wines on a region-by-region basis.

That was some years ago — and led to the first California Living Wine Report in the magazine distributed by the *San Francisco Sunday Examiner & Chronicle*. A second report followed about a year ago. The demand for reprints and the favorable reaction and requests for "more, more . . ." led us to seek new writers, to significantly expand the concept, to put together a new research-writing team — to "make an authoritative, useful book about California wines which has relevance anywhere in the nation — or the world, for that matter."

A great deal of credit has to go to Mildred Howie, who spearheaded the research and the fact-checking, as well as to Harvey Steiman and Robert Thompson, who did much of the writing, but we also consulted others — most notably Herbert Cerwin, Jim Lucas, and Brian St. Pierre, as well as the folks at *Redwood Rancher* magazine, to say nothing of some of the people who helped with the original magazine concept.

That brings us to the title — *Pride of the Wineries* — which stems from one of those never-to-be-forgotten instances that one remembers forever. It happened on a sparkling afternoon in Sonoma County at a barbecue for a wine and food group hosted by the late August Sebastiani, his wife Sylvia, and his son Sam. People were milling around and, as usual, August was the center of attention. Suddenly he said, ever so quietly, "Let's go. I want to show you something." And off we went in his pickup truck. Away from the crowd, down the road to the other side of the vineyard, and to a nearby lake — a pond. August pointed out some of the birds he loved so much. The memorable moment, the image that brought back boyhood memories of farms in rural Maryland, was August Sebastiani reaching over ever so casually, ever so lovingly, and scooping up a double handful of rich dirt that he brought to his face with love and a tinge of awe. It was then that the title *Pride of the Wineries* was conceived.

Harold I. Silverman
Director, California Living Books
Editor In Charge, California Living Magazine

# General
# Introduction

The most prevalent perception of California wine, even in California, is that it begins and ends with the Napa Valley. When a San Franciscan takes a visitor from the East on a day trip to "the wine country," their destination is likely to be somewhere between Oakville and Calistoga. And the truth is that some of the great wines of California do come from the Napa Valley. But stand back and look at the broader picture.

Last year, E. & J. Gallo alone accounted for 42 percent of the total grape crush in California. That is one winery. Between Gallo and Italian Swiss Colony, you have accounted for two-thirds of the wine produced in this state. Or put another way, about half the wine consumed in the United States comes from these two wineries. Gallo bought more than half the total grape harvest in Monterey County last year and substantial portions of the harvest in Napa, Sonoma, Mendocino, and Santa Clara counties as well.

The inescapable conclusion is that Gallo and its fellow large Central Valley wineries are primarily responsible for the economic success of the California wine industry in recent years. They produce a palatable wine, an everyday beverage to drink with meals that is acknowledged — practically unanimously — to be the best *vin ordinaire* the world has ever had.

Nowadays, the Central Valley is going beyond *vin ordinaire*. Improved viticultural techniques have enabled wines of surprising character to be developed in such unlikely places as Delano, Bakersfield, Modesto, and Livingston. Some of the wines being produced there are better than what the Napa Valley was producing just a few decades ago. That's how fast things have improved in California winemaking.

Still, the very finest California wines are produced in the coastal counties, which are cooled by the Pacific fog, rather than in the hot Central Valley. But to keep this in perspective, remember that the total production of Mendocino, Lake, Sonoma, Napa, Solano, Alameda, San Mateo, Santa Clara, Santa Cruz and Monterey counties — the ones the experts generally agree produce the finest wines — accounts for less than 13 percent of the wine produced in California.

But that 13 percent gets a lot of attention. Visit a big liquor store or wine shop in New York or Chicago and you might feel like you're in San Francisco. The walls are lined with bottles from all those very little wineries you thought only Californians had heard of — Freemark Abbey, Spring Mountain, Dry Creek, Chateau St. Jean, Fetzer, Chalone, Firestone, and dozens of others. The number of wineries in California is edging toward four hundred,with the list growing every year,and the competition for the wine drinker's dollar is getting stiffer. That is why wineries today are trying to expand their markets, and why wine drinkers in Chicago, New York, Boston, Miami, and Dallas are discovering that many of the world's great wines come from California. Moreover, they are beginning to discover that California is a collection of quite distinct growing regions. The average Easterner's perception of California viticulture is probably best reflected in a vintage chart published last year in the *New York Times* with separate columns for Bordeaux, red and white; Burgundy, red and white; the Rhine and the Mosel; and then a single column for this side of the Atlantic — California red.

The reality is that Cabernet Sauvignons from the Rutherford district of Napa County have a considerably different character from wines out of the same grape variety grown in Sonoma's Alexander Valley. Gewurztraminers from Sonoma County have considerably more flowery spiciness than wines from the same grape grown in Napa. Zinfandels from San Luis Obispo County tend to be smoother and fruitier than wines from the same grape grown in Napa, which in turn tend to have more depth and roughness. Sonoma Zins have that classic Zinfandel, berrylike character, and Amador Zins run toward bigness — high alcohol and intense varietal character.

These distinctions are only now beginning to be sorted out. Many wineries are labeling their best wines with appellations of origin that pin down more closely where the grapes were grown. The fact that the winery is in Sonoma County is no guarantee that the wine in that winery's bottle is made from Sonoma grapes. Only if the appellation states *Sonoma* can you be certain. Ridge Vineyards, in Santa Clara County, uses grapes from vineyards in Amador, Sacramento, San Luis Obispo, Sonoma, and Napa counties, as well as its own vineyards on Monte Bello Ridge, but each wine's origin is clearly labeled. It was one of the first to do this, though now a legion of wineries are doing the same. At the other extreme is Louis M. Martini. All Martini wines are labeled with a California appellation, yet these wines need take a back seat to no one's. The lesson is that the appellation may tell you something about the character of the wine, but it's no barometer of quality.

If all this seems far too complicated, remember it only applies to some of that 13 percent of California wine made in the coastal counties. Rest assured that you can find a good wine to uncork for Sunday's dinner without going into such detail.

An incredibly high percentage of today's wine is palatable. Before Pasteur, most wines spoiled within a year or two, but Pasteur discovered the microbes that caused wine to spoil and developed winemaking practices to avoid them altogether. Aided by viticultural and enological research in France, Germany, and at the University of California at Davis and Fresno State University, growers and winemakers have the ability to make every bottle of wine drinkable, and pleasantly so.

Never has there been such a range of agreeable wines to choose from, nor available in so many places. The variety of wines on supermarket shelves today exceeds in quantity and quality what was available in some of the best liquor stores just a few years ago. Today a wine shop shelf offers something from just about anywhere wine is made. Most of those wines will probably come from California, since roughly seven out of every ten bottles of wine consumed in the United States is produced in California. Another one of the ten comes from elsewhere in the United States, principally New York. And the remaining two bottles originate somewhere in the rest of the world.

Italy exports more wine to the United States than any other country. The latest figures show Italian wines holding 54 percent of the import market. Most of that is sweet, red Lambrusco type wine, but a significant portion is dry or slightly off-dry white wine from Soave and Verdicchio, a reasonably priced alternative to the more popular but increasingly expensive French white Burgundies.

France used to be the number one exporter of wines to the United States, but that was before Chablis and Pouilly-Fuisse jumped to more than $10 a bottle, with the better wines hitting $15, $20, and up. A series of disappointing vintages, in terms of both quantity and quality, has driven the prices of the better-known French wines beyond reach of the average wine drinker. When prices went up on the 1976 Burgundies from an excellent vintage, there were some grumbles, but serious wine drinkers still bought them. But when the prices jumped again in 1977, an awful vintage, many shops just did not buy. With a standard markup, a bottle of Romanee-Conti would have to sell for more than $100. The same thing has been happening in Bordeaux, where 1975 was the last good vintage. Bordeaux produces ten times as much wine as Burgundy, so the price jumps have been less dramatic but still there.

Against this background, California vintners are somewhat more willing to raise their prices than they may have been. The average price of a bottle of wine has edged up close to 15 percent in the last year. The under-two-dollar wines have been least affected, as the big jumps have been in the middle- and upper-range wines, especially such varietals as Chardonnay, Chenin Blanc, Gewurztraminer, and Johannisberg Riesling. Even French Colombard, formerly thought of as a lovely blending grape but nothing worth bottling alone, is commanding prices of $4 and up from some wineries.

What these wines all have in common is that they are white. The increasing wine consumption in the United States has mostly been white wines, a phenomenon that caught the California wine industry rather flatfooted. As a result, many of the red grape vineyards planted in the early 1970s in anticipation of a continuing wine boom have been hastily grafted over to white grapes, such as Sauvignon Blanc and Chenin Blanc. Still the production cannot keep up with demand, and the price wineries pay for white grapes has escalated sharply. The average price of Chardonnay grapes is expected to top one thousand dollars a ton this year. Growers got more for Chenin Blanc in the Napa Valley last year than they did for Cabernet Sauvignon.

Lou Gomberg, the San Francisco wine industry consultant and analyst, correctly points out that the white-wine boom is really a cold-wine boom. Although white wines as cocktails account for a big portion of the increased consumption, rosés and those sweet Italian Lambruscos, meant to be drunk cold, have been guzzled with abandon too.

Whether red or white, Americans are showing an increasing thirst for wine. Wine consumption in the United States is hovering at about two gallons per capita and rising at an annual rate of more than 10 percent. This means Americans will double their annual consumption of wine by 1990. The sad fallout from this upsurge is that the better wines, which used to be reasonably priced, have become too expensive for most of us. There are alternatives, however, and one of the side effects is that wine drinkers are discovering wines they may never have given a second look. Among French wine drinkers, those who were drinking Pouilly-Fuisse and Chablis before the prices took off are turning to some lesser known areas of

France that are, in many cases, as good as the well-known districts — St. Veran instead of Chablis, for example, or Macon Blanc instead of Pouilly-Fuisse.

An encouraging trend in Europe is the increasing use of technology, especially on the moderately priced wines. Fermentations are beginning to be temperature controlled to retain the natural fruitiness of the grape, and cellar practices are improving, so we get cleaner, more drinkable wines. This is happening in parts of France, Spain, Germany, and especially in Italy. The overall result is more decent wine at decent prices.

In California, the flurry of vineyard planting that took place at the beginning of the seventies is bearing fruit, although the pace has slowed considerably. The stage is set for another surge of investment in new plantings over the next few years. The question is where. All the vineyard land in the Napa Valley is essentially planted. Likewise Sonoma, which has experienced dramatic expansion in the last few years. Mendocino still has room to grow, and Lake County is promising. Monterey County, over-planted in the early 1970s and just now beginning to catch up financially, can grow some more, but the most available acreage in the prime coastal regions is in San Luis Obispo and Santa Barbara counties. The wines being made in these coastal valleys have been winning top medals in recent wine judgings, and local county agricultural agents estimate that there are roughly 50,000 acres suitable for wine grapes yet to be planted there. As for the big-volume wineries, a vice president of one pointed to the Sierra Foothills of Nevada, Placer, El Dorado, Amador, and Calaveras counties as having enormous potential.

Elsewhere in the United States, commercial vineyards and wineries have popped up in thirty states. On the West Coast, Washington and Oregon are beginning to produce notable wines; the most readily available are Chateau St. Michelle of Washington and Tualatin of Oregon. As interesting as these wines are to the curious, in practical terms they are as significant today as wines from Argentina, Chile, South Africa, and Australia. All these countries produce some excellent wines, but by the time they get to us, they have become relatively expensive. Similarly, as good as wines from Oregon, Washington, New York, and Ohio might be, they are, for now, curiosities. Marvin Shanken, publisher of *Impact,* an industry newsletter, doesn't think they'll ever be significant. "I see little future for non-California wineries except for local distribution," he said. "The real future is right here in California."

# Varietal Character

To take California wine seriously is to embark on a quest for varietal character, and it is a quest Don Quixote would have enjoyed. Varietal character, for those who have yet to tilt with this particular windmill, is the characteristic flavor of each individual grape variety. For example, what does the *true* Cabernet Sauvignon or the *true* Chardonnay grape wine taste like? To define these flavors, members of the Department of Viticulture and Enology at the University of California at Davis have evolved a set of flavor associations. Gewurztraminer is spicy. Semillon has the flavor of fresh figs, or — the smell of freshly washed bedsheets drying in the sun. For Chardonnay, the association is apples. Among reds, Cabernet Sauvignon is likened to black tea, herbs, or olives. Pinot Noir recalls mint. Zinfandel is briary or berrylike.

Those are easy ones. Other varieties, alas, are less specific. Chenin Blanc is described as pleasantly fruity — no more. Barbera is just vinous. Philip Wagner, the book-writing grape grower of Maryland, laid it all out in an even less helpful line: "Vinifera grapes are delicate in flavor, tending toward neutral." The complexity of this rich subject gets even more confusing. But fortunately for us it gets more interesting as well.

A few years ago the well-known winemaker Louis P. Martini said that Cabernet Sauvignon grapes don't always make the best Cabernet Sauvignon wine in the world. Sometimes a winemaker can get more varietal character into a bottle by blending in grapes of other varieties that serve to restore something a particular vintage or vineyard left out. For example, rainy 1972 in California washed out a good deal of the tannins that give Cabernet Sauvignon its characteristic pucker in the mouth. Blending in some Petite Sirah, say, can restore the tannins without muddling the typical taste of tea or herbs. Petite Sirah is one of the less distinctive varietals. Sometimes, it is just a question of the essential flavor. A Cabernet weak on herbaceous aromas can be enhanced no little by the addition of Merlot or Cabernet Franc or maybe even Ruby Cabernet or Carignane. This is an unbearable thought to apprentice connoisseurs, who hope that a 100-percent, one-grape-variety wine will help resolve their doubts. But it is quite true nonetheless.

These are the easy obstacles. Varietal character in grapes is naturally altered when the juice ferments into wine, and still more while it ages. Among quality producers, the whole point of winemaking is to preserve varietal character, yet to shade it enough with personal touches so that the wine has a particular winemaker's stamp. And blending is one obvious way to do this. Even without blending, aging in different kinds of wood for varied periods of time can augment varietal character in dozens of different ways. More time in the bottle brings on an additional range of alterations in taste.

Most of these lessons were delivered with perfect clarity when Joe Heitz of Heitz Cellars conducted a tasting of Chardonnays for a roving band of associates from the Smithsonian Institute. He offered some newly crushed 1977 juice, some 1977 must (crushed juice) halfway through its fermentation, a 1976 wine still in the cask, a newly bottled 1975, a 1974, and a well-matured 1973. The unfermented Chardonnay juice was, indeed, powerfully reminiscent of apple. Some who had never heard of the flavor association list made the comparison. That was about the end of it, however, for apples with most of us. The forming alcohol was one distraction. Hints of an oak taste in the finished wine overpowered the notion for others. By the time we got to the bouquet in the 1973 bottle, people were going on about asparagus, pineapple, and honey, to name just a few of many associations.

The Heitz style, as all veteran observers know, is a bold one. One could even say austere. Chateau St. Jean, over the ridge from Napa in the Sonoma Valley, makes a softer, gentler wine. Up in Mendocino, Parducci makes Chardonnay as straightforward as Chardonnay can be made. These are the variables that keep wine buffs muttering to themselves in exasperated fascination. To carry the fascination further, though not necessarily making anything clearer, we will let the winemakers themselves explain what they think some of the major varietals ought to be like.

## Gewurztraminer

Gewurztraminer is the perfect wine for a kite fly. It goes flawlessly with pâté and other picnic fare, and thirty-mile-an-hour winds cannot blow all of its powerful aroma out of the glass. For these same reasons, it is perfect — possibly unbeatable — for learning both varietal character and individual style as it is almost impossible to diminish the varietal character of Gewurztraminer, although winemakers take pleasure in trying. But more to the point, a lollygag afternoon of pâtés, cheeses, and fruit is the appropriate setting for tasting this varietal, better so and easier than at dinner.

In the books, the words used to characterize Gewurztraminer are spicy (*gewürz* translates from German as "spicy"), flowery, and perfumey. When made dry, it can be very spicy indeed, although no one ever has identified exactly which spice. Sweeter, it is flowery or perfumey, and the perfume can be pinned down. A really fine Gewurz in the flush of its youth has an aroma kindred to cold cream. Sweet or dry, it carries a strong family resemblance to Muscat. And sweet or dry are the crucial decisions in Gewurztraminer. Everything the winemaker does after that exaggerates the original choice. The vintners who style Gewurztraminer sweet tend to be the same people who are enchanted with late-harvest-style Rieslings or German wines or both. Joseph Phelps and Chateau St. Jean Wineries are the pointed examples. They, along with Grand Cru, win most of the first places in fairs, blind tastings, and any other form of competition that comes along in this category. Simi contends for honors with them. Most of the bigger cellars — Almaden, Paul Masson, Inglenook — work in the same territory, as do Pedroncelli, Cresta Blanca, Sebastiani, and a few others.

Made right, the sweet Gewurztraminers are "delicate," says Richard Arrowood of Chateau St. Jean. "Made wrong, they are dime-store perfume." Made right involves a highly refined technique using highly refined equipment: cold fermentation in stainless steel tanks, centrifuging or some other fine filtering procedure, and careful aging in steel or glass. Bob Magnani of Grand Cru says that "being death on oxidation is the key. We get our grapes under a blanket of carbon dioxide as soon as they are harvested, and no oxygen gets to them or the wine until somebody pulls the cork on the bottle." When a winemaker struggles against oxygen, he is trying to preserve the taste of the fresh fruit as much as possible. When he leaves some unfermented sugar in the finished wine he doesn't have anything else in mind at all.

Mary Ann Graf, the former winemaker at Simi, says Gewurztraminers she made there "develop in the bottle. They can be very disappointing at about three months, then they begin to come around." Arrowood echoes that. He suggests six to twelve months after release as the ideal time for drinking his Gewurztraminers. Having these wines with a meal is almost out of the question, as far as the winemakers are concerned. They are for afternoon sipping with fruit or cheese.

Dry Gewurztraminers come from winemakers who look more to Alsace than to Germany for their models, or at least look to people who looked to Alsace before them. Louis M. Martini was the pioneer. The newest Christian Brothers Gewurztraminer is in that vein. Mirassou makes another. But most dry Gewurz comes from small — even tiny — cellars: Stony Hill, Villa Mt. Eden, Z-D, and Husch. The maker of dry Gewurztraminer is not so bound to technique and equipment. None makes a point of wood, though some ferment in it. Most do not mind giving their wines a short turn in wooden cooperage so long as it is too old to impart any flavor. The primary factor for them is when the grapes are picked.

A grape grower with an insatiable taste for soft, sweet Gewurztraminer at its most flavorful once observed, "You don't pick on sugar or acid. Oh, you measure — to see when it's getting close. Then you go out in the field every night. One night, you just get drowned in the perfume. If you don't wait for that, you don't get much in the perfume. If you do wait, you pick like hell as soon as you smell the perfume because then you know the acid is going down like a rock."

The dry wine contingent has a dozen different thoughts on this subject ranging almost up to that one. Mike Chelini, the winemaker at Eleanor McCrea's Stony Hill, says, "We go more for a fruity style, not so much spicy or muscaty. That's why these hills are nice. They give you great acid balance." An ideal year at Stony Hill gives 22.5 degrees sugar and .8 total acid in a grape variety notorious for acids down in the .53 range. Gino Zepponi of Z-D, whose grapes come from the Carneros district in southern Napa County, says, "The primary consideration is to get the grape at its maximum flavor. This does not mean high sugar. As a food wine, it should be relatively high acid. That brings out the fruit." Louis P. Martini will risk some acid to get flavor.

The notion of food or no food is probably the key point of difference among the dry stylists — a vexing question, given the ferocious flavor of Gewurztraminer. Dr. Richard Peterson sums it up with a nonanswer. "All wines," he said, "are food wines, or ought to be. What food for this wine then? Which meal? I'd have to think about that. I really don't know." Zepponi has his thought. "You've got to be a Gewurztraminer lover to like dry Gewurz, but with rich fish or curry nothing beats the accompaniment." Dan Mirassou chooses a middle course. "I like to just drink it when people are around, maybe with fruit and cheese. But it's good with dishes with just a slight touch of curry . . . hardly any at all."

Louis P. Martini, who has made more dry Gewurztraminer than the whole rest of the field put together, thinks the wine "completely overpowers food. It's a great appetizer. That's all." His Gewurztraminers are indeed more pungently varietal than any of the other dry editions. For all of Louis

P.'s disclaimers, the wine mates very well with pâtés, choucruote garnie, and other waist-thickening Alsatian fare.

"I like it with a year's bottle age," says Martini, "and eighteen months isn't too much. Two years may be best. After that, you begin to run some chance of it going over the hill. But age varies considerably. If you can pick with good acid, Gewurztraminer will age pretty well. Not too long ago we opened a bottle of 1948. It was still good. It hadn't browned. I'm not sure it still tasted too much of traminer, but it was a very good old white wine."

Few mortals have such patience. "I'm sorry I don't have any old Gewurztraminer around," Eleanor McCrea said one day over a fine salmon mousse at Stony Hill, "but it seems to slide down my gullet so fast there never is any."

## Dry Sauvignon Blancs

Sauvignon Blanc is a chameleon. The wine goes by several names — Sauvignon Blanc, dry Sauvignon Blanc, Fumé Blanc and Blanc Fumé — all are in current use — ostensibly to reflect the many different styles. In truth, there are more styles than names, and the names are freely interchangeable among the styles.

But that's all right because Sauvignon Blanc is a comer among California whites in all of its guises. It can be made for almost instant consumption as a light, fresh, fruity wine by fermenting it cold and not quite dry (and, possibly, by blending away some of its intense varietal character). It can also be made bone dry, tartly austere — with or without a kiss of wood — for long aging. Or it can be made bone dry and full bodied, austere for its characteristic herbaceous flavor rather than uncommon tartness. Again, wood can be in or out of the picture — the winemaker's choice — and aging a better idea than not. Finally it can be made sweet, but that is a subject for another story.

Robert Mondavi Fumé Blanc 1978 is probably the best starting point for thinking about all the things Sauvignon Blanc can be. "First," says Mike Mondavi, "we blend Semillon with the Sauvignon Blanc. We feel 100 percent Sauvignon Blanc is too intense. The Semillon gives the wine a little more complexity and drinkability." The ratio usually is eighty-five to fifteen. The Mondavis choose to pick at relatively high sugars, 22 to 23 degrees on the Brix scale. They have a distinctive fermentation, running about 70 percent through steel tanks, and 30 percent in oak barrels. The barrel-fermented portion then ages on its yeast for eight to nine months before being blended back with the majority. "The reason we do this is for intensity, and the reason we limit it to 30 percent is so we don't get too much." The wine is bone dry.

The Mondavis love their Fumé Blanc best with raw oysters. They care for it almost as much with plain fish, but do not like it so well with fish in sauces. "Sweet or creamy sauces attack the wine's tannins and acids in the absence of residual sugar, so it tastes harsher than it should," says Mike.

A good many others lean in a similar, though less complicated direction. Chateau St. Jean and Joseph Phelps are among these. Almaden, Concannon, Christian Brothers, Inglenook, Charles Krug, San Martini, and Wente Bros. are less marked by oak, and more likely to show a hint of residual sugar, but less than threshold.

At least two major producers lean farther in the direction of fresh, fruity — even sweet. Beaulieu has introduced its first Dry Sauvignon Blanc, a 1976, which exemplifies the possibilities. Winery president Legh Knowles, Jr., says: "We fermented it dry, tasted it, and decided to back up a step. We blended in about 2 percent of a sweet Chenin Blanc to soften the intense varietal character and also to bring the residual sugar just up to threshold. We kept the wine in steel all the way. We wanted it to be fresh and drinkable now." Accent on the now.

Without the supplement of Chenin Blanc and with a touch less sugar, Beringer's 1976 takes a similarly affable tack. The key in all of these is a certain degree of easy pleasure. "The distinct aromatic flavor is so strong," notes an academic survey of California wine grapes, "that in some regions and years it may have to be blended with a more neutral-flavored variety to achieve consumer acceptance."

Four small wineries go the limit in the other direction, of awesome varietal intensity. This quartet either does not agree with the survey or at least is willing to test the limits. "All of our Sauvignon Blancs except 1974 have gone in a line — pungent, grassy, dry," says David Spaulding of Stonegate, near Calistoga. "In tastings people love it or hate it. Among wines it kind of corresponds to a blue cheese." Ric Forman, formerly at Sterling Vineyards, now on his own, echoes that. "For me, it should be extremely herbaceous, like Cabernet Sauvignon — bell peppery, maybe musky. I love them when they're almost smelly." Mike Robbins of Spring Mountain says, "It's pretty much a wine drinker's wine. It's almost an acquired taste. I want to get as much of what I call gun-metal character as we can get. I know nobody eats guns, but there's something of the smell of a gun in a good Sauvignon Blanc."

For all their agreement on the grape's intense character, these three wines and David Stare's Dry Creek Fumé Blanc differ distinctly among themselves, and for good reason. The models and the methods are not the same. Stare does not blend at all. "Ours is 100 percent Sauvignon Blanc. It always has been. I hope I always can say it will be. If you are going to call a wine after a variety it ought to taste as much as possible of the variety." His

1974 remains his favorite because it was and still is the most pungently grassy of his vintages to date. The proprietor of Dry Creek did not pattern his wine after any particular model. "The first year, I simply made wine the best I could. After that the Fumé Blanc just evolved. I'm trying to make a Sonoma County Sauvignon Blanc with a lot of varietal flavor and some smoothness from oak aging."

Spring Mountain's Robbins, another 100 percent advocate, did have a model. "Personally, I got into Sauvignon Blanc from Pouilly-Fumé instead of Graves. My favorite in the old days was Chateau de Tracy. I was very enamored of this wine at one time. At Spring Mountain I wanted to come as close as we could to a very heavy Pouilly-Fumé." In contrast, Forman is "very fond of Graves. It's the hardest of white wines. Tart is what matters. The Sterling blend had about 10 percent Semillon, 15 percent at most. I use Semillon for basically the same reason I blend Merlot with Cabernet Sauvignon. I think there is a nice flavor component that introduces a very pleasing complexity." At Stonegate, Spaulding adds to the philosophical trends, patterning his Sauvignon Blancs on two from 1972 — Spring Mountain and the van Loben Sels bottling from the now-disappeared Oakville Vineyard winery.

Against these differences, all agreed on one point: Aging in oak is very important, but a strong taste of the wood itself is shunned. Stare ages his Fumé Blanc "in French oak for two to four months, depending on the age of the barrel . . . just enough to soften the wine." At Spring Mountain, says Robbins, "we never use new wood if we can avoid it. We like to give the wine six months maximum in Limousin oak that's been used for two or three vintages of Chardonnay." Sterling Sauvignon Blancs are aged, half and half, in three-thousand-gallon oak tanks and sixty-gallon barrels, both of European oak.

The real differences among the wines seem to come mainly from the winemaker's approach to grape ripeness. Forman says, "Sauvignon Blanc has to be good and tart. You can make excellent Sauvignon Blanc with practically any sugar you want, from 20 to 24 degrees, so we pick our grapes to get lots of acid. Acid is the most important." Robbins, on the other hand, says, "The Wentes made some marvelous Sauvignon Blancs picking at 21 or 22 degrees Brix. We don't seem to get the character [in the Napa Valley] at those sugars, so we go from 22 to 23." Spaulding also leans toward 22 degrees and up. Stare has tended to stay with the 21 to 22 degree range, partly because his cooler vineyard does not give much more sugar than that. There is something of a dilemma, says Spaulding. "Pick too early, and there is an underripe taste. But the longer Sauvignon Blanc is left on the vine, the less varietal character the wine has."

As much as they may diverge in the winery, once the wine is in the bottle, all four agree on what to do. Drink the wine with fish, and above all with salmon. The wine also goes well with garlicky dishes, whether there is an underlay of fish or chicken.

## Pinot Noir

To start a verbal free-for-all about California wine, lock any four interested parties in a room and say, "Pinot Noir." Pinot Noir seems to be like the little girl with the little curl who was either very, very good or horrid — and nobody knows why. Recently a veteran winemaker has thrown Pinot Noir out of his list. "It is," says the man, who out of pity shall go unnamed, "a dog." Even people with high hope admit a degree of bewilderment. Rod Strong of Sonoma Vineyards wants his epitaph to say he made a great Pinot Noir, but he says, "The mysteries of Pinot Noir have defied the best efforts of chemists anywhere . . . in explaining the failures of California Pinot Noir . . . or its occasional successes."

Andre Tchelistcheff is something like the patron saint of Pinot Noir in California. During his long career at Beaulieu Vineyards he has made some memorable ones, including one that even satisfied him. It was the 1946, but he has not lost hope in the years since then. What Tchelistcheff says he wants is a grape — and a wine — with "a creaminess, a rich, round, creamy taste. There should be a complexity of texture. The fruit should be excitingly rich, just like an outstanding filet steak, and should have the richness of the meat itself." Tchelistcheff also says a fine Pinot Noir "should have a little, a slight, a barely visible reflection of raisin."

Nobody argues with any of that, and some amplify the thought. Sonoma Vineyards' Strong says a perfect Pinot Noir is signaled by a taste of "luxurious decadence." One could go on, but it should be clear that this is a wine for romantics, for those who chase after stars. With this wine, more than any other, winemakers fuss over the grapes, although they are not in perfect agreement about how to fuss. Strong's Pinot Noir vines grow in California's coolest grape-growing region. "That's very important. Our Pinot Noir is harvested very late . . . the latter part of September to the first week of October. In 1977 we finished in the third week in October. Keeping the fruit on the vine for a long time is the key, so it can ripen very gradually. With heat, the effect is that you lose the subtlety, the elegance of flavor. Also, the cool climate gives substantial color . . . not rosé, as too many Pinot Noirs are."

"The 90-percent factor is climate," says Gino Zepponi of tiny Z-D. "The rest is clones and soils." "More important than climate is soil," says Michael Hoffman of Hoffman Mountain Ranch in the coast hills of San Luis Obispo County. "We have a real chalky, limey soil . . . very gravelly." It is yielding a dark-hued, intensely flavored wine in spite of being in a considerably warmer climate than Sonoma Vineyards. "Clone is the biggest thing," says Bob Sessions, winemaker at Hanzell in Sonoma, the source of some legendary Pinot Noirs.

Pinot Noir is a variety notorious for its genetic frailty and is always on the way to becoming something else. The result is that there are dozens of subvarieties. Matching the right subvariety to its best vineyard site is one of the ongoing preoccupations of Pinot Noir growers. "My first feeling," says Z-D's Zepponi, "is that Pinot Noir should not be made to be like French Burgundy. It is not, should not, and will not be. It can be as elegant, as good, but it is different. This isn't Burgundy. We don't have the growing conditions — climate or topography — and we can't add sugar."

"We just try to get as much as we can out of our grapes," says Michael Hoffman. "Most of our techniques are derivative of Andre's" (Tchelistcheff, consulting enologist to Hoffman Mountain Ranch, who has some direct ties to Burgundy as well as a long career in California). "Pinot Noir still remains as a challenge in California," says Tchelistcheff. "I know we are not making great Pinot Noir yet. Cabernet Sauvignon is great, but it is easy. The challenge of the winemaker is to make a type from Pinot Noir for California. We can make a great Burgundy in California."

People are going to great lengths attempting to do just that. "The first dumb thing I do is remove the chute on the destemmer," says Sonoma Vineyard's Strong. "We collect the stems in a tarp and dump them into the fermenters. We put about 70 percent of the stems back into the fermenting wine to get a Cote d'Or character." At Hoffman Mountain Ranch, about 50 percent of the stems go into the fermenters. "Instead of putting them in whole, we chop them up with a regular old garden composter," says Michael Hoffman. Among other things, the stems add tannin — which the grape tends to lack — and this gives Pinot Noir extra strength.

If there is a consensus about anything, it is that the fermentation should be warmer and quicker than for any other red. Tchelistcheff favors the range 75 to 80 degrees, which takes from four to five days to complete. His protégé at Hoffman Mountain Ranch seeks a peak in the mid-80s each day, then an overnight cooling "to prolong the fermentation so there is greater contact with the skins." Rod Strong of Sonoma Vineyards sets the thermostat at 90.

Color is another worry. "We ferment in one-ton lots and punch the cap down instead of pumping over," says Sessions of Hanzell. So does Zepponi. At Hoffman Mountain Ranch, Michael Hoffman says, "We use a Swiss method. Instead of pumping over, we pump all the juice out of the tank and let the cap settle to the bottom, then pump the whole volume of juice back on top of it. It works pretty well with Pinot Noir, but it's a mistake with Zinfandel. Don't ask me why." In Tchelistcheff's view, the color of Pinot Noir is "light, but very appealing. It is a far worse mistake to blend for color than to accept what is there, because Pinot Noir is too beautiful a flavor to tamper with." The late Karl Wente, who also knew something about grapes, disagreed up to a point. "I walked every row of La Romanee once," he said, "and they have more than one grape variety in there. I'm absolutely convinced that what makes those wines better than the rest is a perfect balance of varieties in the vineyard." His own first stride was to add 10 percent of Pinot St. George to his Pinot Noir. "Pinot St. George is kind of rough and all that, but without it the Pinot Noir just doesn't have enough strength or complexity."

Petite Sirah is the usual blending grape, since it adds both color and tannin. Tchelistcheff's old outfit, Beaulieu, has both a pure Pinot Noir (Beaumont) and one blended eight to twenty with Petite Sirah (Beau Velours). The Beaumont also gets a considerably longer wood aging. A third offering to make a comparative tasting should be Sebastiani Pinot Noir, which is strengthened with a proportion of Petite Sirah and which gets a long aging in wood. Any further wines for comparison should come from a 100-percent Pinot Noir field that includes Chalone and San Martin from Monterey County, Mt. Eden from Santa Clara County, Robert Mondavi from Napa, and the Sonomans already noted.

Most Pinot Noirs in their prime fit in perfectly with rich filet steaks, an echo of Tchelistcheff's thought about how the grapes should taste — or better, feel — even before they ferment. Rod Strong's notion of luxurious decadence also points in the direction of well-aged beef. Bob Sessions of Hanzell thinks a good year, for example 1973, "is big enough to stand up to a leg of lamb." Picking good individual wines within this variety is not easy. Every winemaker dismisses more vintages than he likes. Strong, for example, feels that his 1974 Estate Bottled is the first to begin to be what he has been working towards for all these years.

## *Chardonnay*

Chardonnay is California's greatest grape and wine. The honors to Chardonnay come in droves because the grape almost demands to be made into a rich, savory white wine with remarkable aging powers. It readily lends itself to all the favorite yardsticks of greatness connoisseurs use in their endless verbal jousts, and it still manages to taste good.

Considering that Chardonnay is a wine of profound character, pinpointing its varietal flavor is not easy. In the vineyard, it is reminiscent of apple flavors, and wine made without wood aging can keep that flavor alive. But fermentation or aging in wood, or both, usually hides the apple beneath waves of other flavors. The description that surfaces most often is buttery, or — close — creamy. And still, even though few words come to mind that define the character precisely, Chardonnay on the tongue remains one of the easiest wines to identify in a blind tasting.

Ric Forman of Forman Winery reflects on the difference between Sauvignon Blanc and Chardonnay. Sauvignon Blanc, with a sharply defined but fairly simple flavor, "is a very individual wine. The range of styles is enormous." On the other hand, because it has subtle strengths, "Chardonnay is pretty much always Chardonnay, no matter what you do."

In all but a few cases the winemaker gets down to either of two main choices: strength versus delicacy of varietal character, and balance between fruit and wood flavors. The shadings can be very fine indeed. Strength versus delicacy is largely resolved in the vineyard, although the Chardonnay grape shows a rare ability to be itself in a wide range of climates and soils.

Joe Heitz of Heitz Cellars, who has made some legendary contributions, starts off any discussion by saying, "I like lots of guts in all my wines." The source of Chardonnay that has suited him best to date is a piece of Napa Valley bottomland on Zinfandel Lane near the Napa River. He still says "The 1968 Lot-Z is the best wine I ever made," although the 1973 crowds its older brother for first place. Bob Travers of Mayacamas likes strength too. "High ripeness is the single most important factor in the round, viscous Chardonnays I like. The alcohol has to be well over 13 percent to give the extract you need for that kind of character. We're always right against the 14-percent limit." His vines are planted high up in the Mayacamas Mountains on the crest of a ridge.

A long way south in the Gavilan Range, in Monterey County, Dick Graff of Chalone echoes the Napans about strength in Chardonnay, but insists on regional identity. "There's a *gout de terroir* from Chalone. It's particularly noticeable as wines age. You don't hear too much talk about soil in California, I think because the differences can't be measured in the lab. But the character of the wine comes from there. It's similar to *timbre* in music. Our wines have a certain character because of the place they're grown." Dick Arrowood, of Chateau St. Jean in the Sonoma Valley, also has high regard for the characteristics of individual vineyards, even within a small district. He makes as many as seven different Chardonnays from a single vintage, most from particular vineyards. "The reason I make so many is I believe there are major differences from one vineyard to another. I've proved to myself over the last three years that the vertical similarities are impressive. Each vineyard's fingerprints seem to come out no matter what the vintage is like. I know I can spot the vineyards in blind tastings. I think a lot of consumers could do a lot of sorting too."

There is some variety of opinion about the fermentation process. Most use stainless steel and hold the temperature in the 50-degree range. Graff ferments in small wood, keeping the cellar cool but applying no refrigeration directly to the wine. Arrowood starts in steel, then transfers the wine to barrels for the last of the process.

However, it is aging that occupies the minds of the winemakers most fully. Both the choice of wood and the length of time the wine is aged weigh heavily. "I like enough oak," says Mayacamas's Travers, "to know I'm actually tasting oak. It contributes to the oiliness, the richness of good Chardonnay. You never hit the oak exactly right," he says. "You get a little too much or a little too little . . . about half and half. We use only French wood. We tried a little bit of American oak, but didn't find one we liked." "Oak," says Joe Heitz, "ought to be used like a fine cook uses ingredients in a sauce. You should always be aware of a complex flavor being present but never quite sure what all has gone into it." Arrowood expresses a similar thought differently. He uses barrels from three separate French sources — Limousin, Nevers, and Troncais — but does not want the wine "so oaked out there's no benefit in it. I want a hint of wood and heaps of fruit."

Eleanor McCrea at Stony Hill, famous for the delicacy of its Chardonnay, does not want anyone to taste oak as an identifiable flavor in her Chardonnay, although it is fermented and aged in wood. The secret: "Well-seasoned puncheons." Puncheons are roughly twice the size of barrels. Most of the makers of "big" Chardonnays use each barrel for three to five vintages, then they replace it. At Stony Hill, a five-year-old puncheon is just hitting its stride.

It is even possible to ignore oak altogether. Wente Bros. does, or comes very close to it. So does John Parducci of Parducci Wine Cellars in Mendocino County. His reasons are complicated and not absolute. "I want to get into the Cadillac class," he says. However, "there's no track record up here. I have my feelings about where to plant and how to make the wine. You'll know when I find enough good grapes. The wine will come out under our Cellarmaster label, and it will compete with all those big damn wines." Meantime the Chardonnays that appear under the regular Parducci label are styled "to steal a little thunder from Pouilly-Fuisse. The majority of people on the street prefer fruity no-oak wines. We used a little oak with our 1975. We ran more than a hundred tastings around the country, and the 1974 and 1976 always came in ahead of it. With the grapes we've had up to now, we have been able to make very steady quality of 100 percent Chardonnay that is good value. We ferment cold and minimize our processing, and sell the wine when it is fresh and young. But, next year . . ."

Wente Bros. and Paul Masson are almost the only others who work in this woodless way. Almaden, Beringer, Christian Brothers, and other sizeable firms show some oak. The smaller houses including Hanzell — where oak had its modern beginnings in Chardonnay — Dry Creek, Freemark Abbey, and others, all use oak.

The lighter, less oaky wines want early consumption — within three years — and are cheerful companions to all manner of foods. The big, oak-kissed wines want time and more particular circumstances. Dick

Graff of Chalone says Chardonnay "takes about five years to mature. Ours would be fine for another ten, fifteen, twenty years . . . I don't know. We don't have any old enough to know. The 1960 at fifteen was just delicious." To go with it? "Something like chicken breast with a fairly elegant sauce . . . very fine, but also very rich." Bob Travers of Mayacamas says, "Generally I like our Chardonnays best when they're four to six years old. But the 1971 is in amazingly good shape. So is the 1970." His choice of companion to a fine bottle is down to one. "No question. Live Maine lobster." Dick Arrowood says, "Our wines are not going to peak before three to seven years. Some of them are going to last as long as reds. As far as food, crab and lobster are great, but I love Chardonnay by itself. I would much rather sit in front of a fire with some bread and cheeses and just drink."

## Zinfandel

The late August Sebastiani once made the definitive statement about Zinfandel: "It's so good you want to drink it every day, but not so great it wears you out." This pronouncement holds, though the grape is abundant in every winegrowing district of the state and many winemakers have aimed at turning out wines that are weighty by any standard, from this widely planted grape.

To begin at the beginning, Zinfandel is naturally delicious. The flavor association is blackberry to a lot of people, raspberry to an even greater number. Either way, the sense is of a tart, fresh, wild-fruit taste — an intense, but straightforward wine. Given this agreeable beginning, winemakers can retain as much of the varietal flavor as possible or turn towards oak aging and other techniques for adding complexities. This grape has no European counterpart to fret about, therefore there is virtually no need to see what is going on in Beaune, or wherever. The spirit can be very blithe indeed, and it usually is.

Louis P. Martini has one of the longest histories with Zinfandel in the state and one of the best reputations for doing the right thing for this grape variety. "We make our Zinfandel just like we make any other red . . . leave it on the skins the normal time during fermentation, down to about 6 to 8 percent sugar. Sometimes I go by that. Sometimes I go by days. Four days on the skins is the most we allow. The good ones come out in the vicinity of 13 to 13.5 percent alcohol, quite dark, very fruity, with exceptionally good aging capacity. In our vineyard, quality correlates inversely to the crop . . . more so than with some of the other varieties. When we have an oversized crop, we get pleasant wine, but thinner, without the aging capacity of wines from short crops. We use primarily large tanks to preserve the fruitiness as much as possible. There's no attempt to keep it in small wood of any kind."

Martini has a program of special selection Zinfandels from slightly riper grapes, yielding slightly higher alcohols. These ferment longer on the skins, for a darker color and more tannin. This is a road on which a good many others have embarked. Paul Draper at Ridge has spent more time on it than anyone else. "The majority of Zinfandels seem to be most interesting when made somewhere between a fully ripe Claret style and a late harvest," Draper said. That means about 14 percent alcohol. Draper, like Martini, looks for a short crop, between one and three tons per acre. Unlike Martini he ferments "on the skins an average of twelve days. The final day lets the last residual sugar work itself out. We *do* go dry." After malo-lactic fermentation, Ridge Zinfandels age . . . "depending on the individual wine . . . from a year and a half to two years in small oak. There's no big cooperage."

"Maybe it's chauvinism," Draper said, "but I prefer air-dried American oak for both Cabernet Sauvignon and Zinfandel. I always use a small amount of new barrels and a large proportion of two- and three-year-old barrels so we don't get too much oak." When Draper uses the plural in referring to Ridge Zinfandels he means it. The label shelters at least three each year, each from a different region. Some years there are more. The regions have "their separate charms," he says. "Amador County wines made in a Claret style can be quite elegant. They have a distinctive regional fruitiness. Monte Bello, from this mountain [west of Cupertino in Santa Clara County], has a unique intensity of spiciness. The wines from Sonoma — I'm really talking about our Geyserville — are some of our richest and consistently most complex Zinfandels. The fifty-five-year-old Dusi vineyard at Paso Robles is spice and herbs." Louis Martini echoes Draper's pleasure in a wide range of regional styles, although he will make a first choice, (his Monte Rosso vineyard at Sonoma), something that Draper cannot bring himself to do.

A man with a single-minded interest in just one region is Richard Peterson of the Monterey Vineyard. "Quality wine," he said, "requires quality grapes, which usually means ripe grapes grown under the coolest conditions possible." This, for Peterson, means the El Camino Ranch near Gonzales in the Salinas Valley, source of his "December Harvest" Zinfandels. By mid-November of 1974, the sugar reached 24 degrees (enough to give more than 14 percent alcohol), but the total acidity refused to descend to tolerable levels. Peterson finally picked at 25.2 degrees sugar and .9 percent acid (compared to a normal 23 degrees and 1.0 percent for Martini). The date was December 5.

"It was," Peterson said, "the first time I've ever had to ignore sugar and use acidity as the prime index of grape ripeness." He had to do it again in 1975, missed in 1976, and got only a small lot in 1977. "The skins of December Harvest Zinfandel grapes are intensely flavorful. That carried through fermentation. The wines age in American oak for a year, which is longer than our regular Zinfandel. They just have to have extra time in new, small barrels. Strangely, a December Harvest has more flavor than tannin. In spite of the high sugar and slow maturation, it is not heavy or alcoholic in the way of wines called 'Late Harvest.' "

The freshest eye for Zinfandel in the state belongs to Bernard Portet. Born in Bordeaux and a winemaker there until 1972, he launched Clos du Val the same year in the Napa Valley and immediately joined the ranks of big, rich Zinfandel makers. "Zinfandel appeals to me most with high alcohol . . . 13.6, 13.8 . . . the 1974 is 14.1 percent. I think you get the most out of the variety at that alcohol level. In 1972 I made two lots. One was heavy, harsh and tannin. It took me six months to make up my mind what to do."

If there was a maverick about Zinfandel, it was August Sebastiani. At least he was less bound by the rules than anybody else when he thought the wine wanted unusual treatment. He, like Louis Martini, wanted to keep a lot of fruit and did not like any oak flavor at all. Yet he had aged some Zinfandels in big tanks for as long as four years. "It depends entirely on the wine," he said. "When it is smooth and mature, we take it out and bottle it. We want the wine to be perfectly drinkable when the consumer gets it."

For the other winemakers, blending with other varieties is nonexistent or minimal. Martini has, on rare occasions, softened over-sharp Zinfandels with a soupçon of Gamay. Draper has allowed a little Petite Sirah in some of his Zinfandel when it came that way from an interplanted vineyard. For Sebastiani, blending was not sought, but it would be tolerated. "We never blend Zinfandel in the sense of buying grapes to do that. It is complete within itself and doesn't need that. But we buy vineyards. If they have Petite Sirah or Carignane in 'em, that's the way it goes. We like Zinfandel from old vines . . . even if they aren't all Zinfandel vines. Some of those guys who planted a long time ago knew what they were doing."

The one point of agreement seems to be how long to hang on to a Zinfandel. Paul Draper of Ridge says, "They reach a plateau something like five years out. They continue to improve after that, but more slowly. If a Zinfandel is well made with tannin, with good acid, it's definitely going to be around fifteen years or more." Louis Martini thinks six to ten years is right. "Younger, they are nice, but too young . . . they have too many corners on 'em. After ten years they can increase in quality, but they taste less and less like Zinfandel. It's all bottle bouquet. At six to ten there is still lots of fruit. That's the most pleasant time to drink them as Zinfandels."

Even the outside range seems agreed. Martini has "some '47s that are still on the plateau, still excellent." Peterson looks for his December Harvest to "be a thirty-year wine." Draper agrees, citing a tasting of eight Zinfandels made between 1938 and 1941 — not "conscientiously designed as fifty-year wines, but all still in excellent shape . . . really complex and elegant."

As for what food to have with them, there is again considerable agreement. "It's versatile," says Draper, ". . . anything from good homemade pasta to . . . to . . . put it this way: preferably I have it with fairly rich, full-flavored food. The Zinfandels I prefer are spicy and rich enough to overpower delicate dishes." Louis Martini said, "It goes with about anything. Probably I prefer it with stews and pastas. It's really good with stews. It's not that good with straight roast beef. I'd rather have Pinot Noir there."

The state is full of people who think seriously about Zinfandel. Most of the rest fall within the range suggested by Martini at the fresher, subtler end and Draper at the big, chewy end of the scale. Bob Trinchero at Sutter Home makes Amador Zinfandels that offer a striking comparison to their counterparts from Ridge, partly for similarities, partly for differences. Trinchero uses redwood tanks as well as oak. The brothers Pedroncelli in Sonoma County provide a graceful bridge between Martini and Sebastiani. Walt Raymond of Raymond Vineyard, having grown up in a different place, produced a debut 1974 Zinfandel that relates to Portet's 1974 Clos du Val much as Sutter Home compares with Ridge Fiddletown. The list could get to be a telephone book, and the modest prices of most Zinfandels encourage bold and pleasurable exploration.

## Chenin Blanc

Chenin Blanc has been and will likely continue to be California's best hammock wine. Its round, fruity charms are perfect for afternoon sipping, especially when there is a perceptible sweetness to enhance the flavor. The wine was invented twenty-odd years ago at Charles Krug in the Napa Valley. Before then, wine from this grape variety almost invariably was made dry and called White Pinot. Its reputation was as a type of lesser white Burgundy.

The Cesare Mondavi family at Krug worked out the techniques for keeping it just slightly sweet. The model was Vouvray, and the wine was a roaring success. Although dozens of other off-dry Chenin Blancs of good to outstanding quality populate the market these days, the Krug is still a good place to go for lesson number one.

"Essentially we ferment now in glass-lined tanks in refrigerated rooms," says Peter Mondavi. "Real good refrigeration is the big thing. If you don't have to touch the wine, you're ahead. But we still ferment some in the old redwood tanks with cooling coils in them, just like we did back at the beginning. Even if you use the circulation method of cooling, you can come out fine. You just have to be extra careful."

Mondavi and the crew at Krug look for grapes at 21 to 23 degrees sugar, maximum. "What we really want is an average 22 degrees. When we get that, good acid will come along. We're not really looking at total acid, though. We're looking at sugar. We'll take what we get on acid. Then in fermenting, we want to end up about 1.5 to 1.75 percent residual grape sugar. [Note: .5 percent sugar is the point at which most people begin to perceive a sweet taste.] It depends on the season. We go by taste, but it almost always ends up somewhere in there. We start watching at about 2 percent, then arrest by taste. We stop the fermentation by chilling, then by filtering out the yeasts.

"We still keep the wine in wood for a short time. We don't have to. We're looking for fresh fruitiness. There's a little bit of a difference between wine that stays in the glass-lined steel tanks all the way and the wine we put in tanks for two or three months, but it's not very much. It's just like in the fermenting. You have to be extra careful. But the wine can come out fine either way."

Mondavi thinks his Chenin Blanc is "at a prime at about nine months old." As for matching it with food, "I'd say number one would be fish, just as a personal choice. But it all depends on individual taste. It's very versatile. I can enjoy it with almost any meal."

There are some minor variations among other producers of off-dry Chenin Blancs elsewhere in Napa, Sonoma, and Mendocino counties, but there are not many surprises. Elsewhere, however, it is possible to make Chenin Blanc into something altogether different than a Vouvray-like wine of gentle charms. Monterey County's cooler reaches will yield a tart Germanic wine from the variety without any extra effort by the winemaker. In contrast, the region from there south can be pushed in the same direction though growing conditions get almost as warm as in Napa or Sonoma. Mirassou Vineyards and San Martin are the prime cases in point.

The Mirassou wines of the early 1970s were very tart indeed, with total acids in the range of 1.0 to 1.12 percent. "This," says Steve Mirassou of the 1977, "was our eleventh vintage. We're just learning to grow grapes there. We're getting the Chenin Blanc a lot riper. The wines now are not as high acid. We pick at 22 to 24 degrees of sugar, and get .8 to .9 percent total acid. So we run about 2.25 to 2.75 percent residual sugar, depending on the acid . . . on the year. The lower total acid fits more people. We ferment cold, around 58 degrees Fahrenheit, centrifuge [to stop the fermentation], then put the wine back into steel and keep it around 55 degrees until we bottle. Usually that's between late December and early February."

At San Martin, Ed Friedrich draws on vineyards that ripen a little more easily than those of Mirassou. The principal source is San Martin's own vineyard near King City, in the warmer, sunnier southern end of the Salinas Valley. He also draws on vines east of San Luis Obispo. "We harvest a little earlier," he says, "at about 21 to 21.5 degrees sugar. This gives us acids of .75 to .85 percent."

However, this only explains part of Friedrich's soft Chenin Blanc. Friedrich is German by birth. He was trained there, and most important, his palate was shaped there. "Alcohol has a numbing effect on the taste buds. It also is domineering. By reducing the alcohol, we bring forth more of the grapes," he says. Most Chenin Blancs run in the range of 12 to 13 percent alcohol. Soft Chenin Blanc sticks close to 10 percent.

In addition to picking at lower than average sugars, Friedrich says, "We reduce the alcohol by stopping the fermentation prematurely . . . keeping about 3.2 grams per liter. All of the balances are by taste, but this is usually it. We ferment in stainless steel at 50 to 55 degrees, until we are about 2 to 3 percent above the final residual sugar level, then we drop the temperature to 35 degrees to stop the fermentation. There is very little aging. I want a very distinct varietal character, and with that a strong fruitiness, a berryish taste of the grape. Aging means oxidation and getting old, so we put it in the bottle as soon as possible, around December. The wine never sees a stick of wood."

For all that the Mirassou has higher alcohols, the proprietors use it in much the same way as Friedrich uses soft Chenin Blanc. Says Steve Mirassou, "I love the wine when it comes off the bottling line. It's a little bit raw, but that's the fun. It's so fruity and lively. Six months really rounds it up, rounds the sugar. As far as recommending it with food, I look for something with sauces." Friedrich, on the other hand, prefers his soft Chenin Blanc with Chinese food.

Although the off-dry school dominates now, a hardcore band clings to the older notion of dry Chenin Blanc. Chappellet, Dry Creek, Louis M. Martini, Sterling Vineyards, and Villa Mt. Eden come to mind as the proponents. There is not much precedent elsewhere in the world for this dry style; these local productions are original.

Donn Chappellet says, "We chose to make Chenin Blanc in a big, dry style, somewhat along the lines of what a Chardonnay might be. We let the grapes get a little riper than average, then we take the wine to complete dryness." When he was at Sterling Vineyards, Ric Forman took the specific extra step of adding a touch of Chardonnay to his Chenin Blancs.

Jim McWilliams, proprietor of Villa Mt. Eden, does not go that far. "Our Chenin Blanc follows no particular model. It is dry out of personal preference. I think the grapes on our property [near Oakville] have a natural fruitiness that is enough. The wine is not flinty dry. In fact, some people even think it's a bit sweet."

All dry editions of Chenin Blanc ferment cold in stainless steel, just as their sweeter brethren do. The difference is that the fermenting goes to dry instead of being stopped early. The other major difference in these cellars is that — unlike most of the off-drys — the dry models take a short turn in wood. The purpose is not to gain flavor, but to soften the rough edges of youth.

"We put [Villa Mt. Eden Chenin Blanc] into thousand-gallon tanks," McWilliams says. "The tanks are new, not neutral yet. The taste of oak will dim as they season. We're not after oak. It's a wine for early consumption." Donn Chappellet echoes the thought. "Our Chenin Blanc gets very little wood. We don't want it to have a wood character. Mainly it ages in steel. The wine might be in wood three weeks." The wood is well-seasoned French oak. Louis Martini uses ancient tanks, sometimes redwood, sometimes oak ovals.

The resulting wines are savory with the fruit flavor of Chenin Blanc but unadorned with wood or other bouquet. What does this wine go best with? "I've enjoyed it," says Chappellet, "with light fish and with steak. It's kind of middle-of-the-road in that sense. It has a lot of tolerance. I guess broiled chicken would be about as ideal a food as you can find." McWilliams favors his "with light fish dishes. We use it to cook clams and mussels sometimes, then we drink it with the finished dish."

No one recommends hanging on to a Chenin Blanc for long. McWilliams thinks his "is quite good within a year. It will improve with bottle age — 1974 was our first year, and there's no deterioration in it. They can last if the acid balance is quite good." Chappellet agrees. His, he says, "is probably at its best when it's about two years old. It would hold for another year. Beyond two-and-a-half or three years, and I start to get a little concerned. Some keep. It depends on the acid."

## Cabernet Sauvignon

Give it its head and Cabernet Sauvignon is a wine for people who like to sleep on the ground, play rugby, climb mountains, eat brussels sprouts, and do other things in which some punishment is a part of the pleasure. The characteristic flavor of the grape variety is almost always linked to strong food flavors: green olives, herbs, green peppers. On top of that, Cabernet Sauvignon is among the richest of the red wine grapes in tannins, the compounds that make us pucker up. Made for all it is worth, Cabernet Sauvignon is a connoisseur's choice for memorable meals built around game meats, pepper steaks, and beef in strong sauces. It is also a wine that connoisseurs will age for a long time so some of its strength softens.

Such strengths elicit strong responses from the winemakers in turn. Some reach for the strengths; some try to hide the hard edges altogether. Most try to temper the grape's fierce nature without exorcising it altogether. All of this makes Cabernet Sauvignon a perfect wine for personal statements of style.

Back in the old days, when only a few imbibers had gotten over Prohibition enough to prefer Cabernet Sauvignon to gentler wines, Beaulieu Vineyard, Inglenook, and Louis M. Martini set up the basic dividing lines. The old Inglenook Cabernets of John Daniel and George Deuer — especially the special Cask bottlings — were fermented for an abundance of tannin, then aged in large oak casks to preserve their ferocity. At Beaulieu Vineyard, Andre Tchelistcheff fermented for tannin and strong varietal character all right, but he aged the Georges de Latour Private Reserve in American oak barrels for more than two years to soften and round off the wine before bottling it. Louis M. Martini fermented less for tannin than balance. And, if the herbaceous flavor of Cabernet Sauvignon got out of hand, he would blend in something — in those days mostly Zinfandel — to tone it back a bit. As at Inglenook, the Martini Cabernets aged in large, relatively neutral wood. Some of the time it was redwood; most of the time it was old oak ovals.

European oak barrels have come along in the years since. So have Merlot and other Bordeaux blending grapes. But the main outlines remain surprisingly valid. The de Latour Cabernet of Beaulieu continues to be made to the old standards. For comparison, the same winery also offers a regular Cabernet Sauvignon fermented to a gentler profile and aged for less time in wood. Yet a third — BeauTour — is made much along the lines of the regular; then it is softened still more with a 15 to 20 percent blending of Merlot. The three wines taken together are a textbook lesson in style.

Joe Heitz of Heitz Cellars has extended the old notion of fermenting the wine for strength, then aging it for gentility, especially with his Martha's Vineyard bottlings. "Wood," says Heitz, "mellows wine better than anything. I like wines you can drink. I frequently use the comparison that bottling a wine too soon is like taking a bright kid out of grade school and putting him straight into college without any high school. If you bottle a wine too soon, it can't reach its full potential. It hasn't been prepared." There is no blending. "I'm trying desperately to make a first-quality California Cabernet Sauvignon. I'm not trying to make an imitation Bordeaux with Merlot and all that," Heitz says.

Much of the complexity in Heitz reds comes from a melange of wood cooperage used for aging. "I use redwood, American oak, and French oak. As I've said before, I think wood is to winemaking what seasonings are to cooking. You shouldn't be able to pick out specific wood flavors any more than you can pick out individual seasonings in a really fine sauce. The big trick for me is to use redwood without having the wine taste of redwood. Redwood tires your palate."

Typically, a Martha's Vineyard bottling of Cabernet Sauvignon goes into glass three and a half years after the harvest. Why so long? "That's the way it used to be done. I liked those wines, so I do things the way they used to be done." And why Martha's Vineyard? "The grapes taste better. It's a happy collection of circumstances . . . clonal selection that happens to fit that soil and climate . . . a vineyard that's well cared for and harvested at full maturity. The wine gets no different care in the winery than other Cabernets."

The fact that the individual vineyards do stand out has been more true for the California Cabernets than for any other varietal. In many cases the proof of the pudding is in wineries where a particular vineyard's wine is made like all the others, yet it emerges with a distinct personality.

At Ridge, Paul Draper pursues some of the ancient ideals of Claret (that is to say, old-fashioned Medocs) with some American twists. At the heart of this ideal is his insistence on keeping the cap of grape solids with the fermenting juice until the wine is bone dry — then keeping it there a little while longer. "We ferment on the skins an average of twelve days, but have gone as many as fifteen. We do go dry. When you finish the fermentation cool, as the French traditionally did, you get all of the sugar."

Such fermentations yield the maximum possible natural tannins in the wine. Not many contemporary winemakers follow this course, because wines made this way may want fifteen, even twenty, years of cellaring to come around. Rod Strong at Sonoma Vineyards is one of the few who does it too; although only with the estate bottling from his Alexander's Crown Vineyard on a high hill of the Alexander Valley. Draper also uses a high hill vineyard, Monte Bello, which surrounds the winery in the hills above Cupertino.

Beyond these similarities lie some intriguing differences. First is climate. Monte Bello is cool, Region I. Alexander's Crown is a good deal warmer, on the borderline between Regions II and III.* Second, Draper ages his Cabernet two years, more or less, in American oak — "It may be chauvinism, but I prefer air-dried American oak" — while Strong moves the Alexander's Crown through Nevers oak from France.

Warren Winiarski at Stag's Leap Wine Cellars has settled into a program somewhere between that of Heitz and those of Draper and Strong. "The Golden Rectangle," he says, "gives the greatest possible unity with the greatest possible diversity in one figure. I want to try to hit in taste

---

*California grape-growing areas are broken down into five climatic regions ranging from the coldest to the warmest on an average basis. Region I is the coldest and includes growing areas near Napa, Salinas, Santa Cruz, and Santa Rosa. Region II, central Napa Valley, Sonoma Valley, Santa Clara Valley, and central Salinas Valley, is only slightly cooler. Region III, moderately cool, is representative of the northern Napa Valley, central Salinas Valley, and the Livermore area. Areas near the towns of Ukiah, Davis, Lodi, and Cucamonga characterize warm Region IV. Region V is very warm and includes most of the northern Sacramento and central and southern San Joaquin valleys.

what that does for the eye. That is, I want to match apparently opposite components — hard and soft — into a harmonious unit."

This means several things. First, "That supple, fleshy grape flavor has to be out front. If you get too much wood tannin, you get dry, skeletal dust. I went to a tasting of 1953 Clarets, and they all were bones in a closet." Winiarski picks over his Cabernet Sauvignon vineyard as many as six times in a season to get fully ripened fruit. Technically, the balance is more than 23 degrees sugar, with .7 total acid. But the grapes "get a particular taste when they are ready to pick, and a softness."

"The fermenting wine is separated from skins and seeds when 3 to 6 percent of the grape sugar remains unfermented. [This is fairly typical of costly Cabernets.] After primary and malo-lactic fermentation, a Stag's Leap Cabernet takes a short turn in large cooperage while tartrate crystals form and fall out; then it spends plus or minus fourteen months in French barrels and puncheons of varying ages — just enough time to begin modifying the lush fruit flavor. Mostly we want that to come with time in the bottle." Abstract principle plays no part in Winiarski's decision to blend or not to blend — only taste counts. Some vintages are pure Cabernet. Some have a small fraction of Merlot. "If it is a more perfect creature for having been blended, let it be."

Next door, Bernard Portet of Clos du Val insists on some Merlot. "What appeals to me in Cabernet Sauvignon is wines with lower alcohols than most. Also," says Portet: "I prefer to taste wines younger than anybody. I like to see the life in a wine. I can see what it is going to be, but I am pretty much against tasting a wine when it is too old. Clos du Val's position is not to imitate anybody," the French-born and trained Portet goes on, "but I make wine more in a Pomerol or St. Emilion style even though I am from the Medoc." That is, he seeks a softer kind of tannin, a more youthfully appealing wine. It is for this reason that he uses 15 percent Merlot, sometimes a bit more.

Because his fermentation and aging programs are very similar to Winiarski's, and because the vineyards are side by side, the glorious difference between the two wines must hark back to ripeness in the vineyard. Portet says, elaborating on his wish to keep alcohols in check: "My 1973 is a bit too low. It is not mature by California standards. It is pale. It is taking a long time to develop. The 1974 is more ripe. The 1974 is exactly what I like in Cabernet Sauvignon."

Questions of age-worthiness do not, curiously, parallel the differences in winemaking techniques. As a matter of fact, they are almost constant. Portet says his 1974 will not be perfect for another five years. "Five years from now, I will tell you if it will last another five years." Heitz — like most — says, "Cabernet Sauvignons peak at different times for different people, so, as far as the wine is concerned, the peak becomes a plateau. But, assuming reasonably good conditions all around, a Martha's Vineyard probably would be approaching its optimum seven or eight years after the harvest and should last another ten to fifteen after that before it fades significantly." In 1978, Strong of Sonoma Vineyards put his 1974 Alexander's Crown bottling "another three to five years from its peak."

Most winemakers think of Cabernet Sauvignon as a versatile wine with food — strong foods in its strong youth, subtler ones as the wine ages into its fullest harmonies. Heitz is the exception, though only for his own taste: "Rare prime rib. Everything else is downhill. I don't like to get carried away matching wine and food, but there are a couple and this is one. It seems a shame to waste Martha's Vineyard on anything else."

## *Botrytis*

Most all California Johannisberg Riesling used to be dry, bone dry, and you needn't have much gray hair to remember when such notions as *auslese* were completely foreign. But times have changed. And as usual in California, they have changed in a trice. Where there was none in 1968, there now is enough of the Californian equivalent of *auslese, beerenauslese,* and even *trockenbeerenauslese* for Roosevelt Grier to have a swim. (He won't. At the price, only an oil man could — or would.)

The German names reflect precise requirements for grape sugar in the freshly crushed juice. Those sugar levels in turn reflect ever-increasing levels of infection by what's been called the noble mold, *Botrytis cinerea.* Botrytis has the remarkable ability to dry up the grape, thus concentrating the grape's qualities. California cannot use the German terms but does not yet have its own set of names, so many labels state the residual sugar in a wine. Roughly speaking, equivalents to *spatlese* have 2 to 4 percent residual sugar; counterparts to *ausleses* range from 5 to 8; the equals of *beerenausleses* range from 10 to 15; and the local answers to *trockenbeerenausleses* go from there up to a startling 27 percent.

With residual sugar, the usual berrylike note of the White Riesling acquires an overtone of apricot. As the sugar goes up, that flavor intensifies until it dominates. The sweetest will cloy when not enough noble mold is present to concentrate the grape acids and add its own sharp flavor as a balance. When everything does go right, the wine is too good to serve to mere kings. It should only go to the best of your friends, presuming they know wine and love sweet. The plural is important as you will need two or three friends. One bottle of such ambrosia goes a long way.

Wente Bros. made the first stab at these wines in the vintage of 1969, calling the result *spatlese.* After a lull there came a few challengers in 1972, a flock of equals and superiors in 1973, then a veritable flood from 1975 onward.

All sorts of folks have equivalents of *spatleses* and *ausleses*. Of the seekers after *beerenauslese* and *trockenbeerenauslese* styles, the foremost are Chateau St. Jean (Selected Late Harvest, Individual Bunch Selected Late Harvest), Freemark Abbey (Edelwein, Edelwein Gold), and Joseph Phelps (Selected Late Harvest). Challengers are coming, notably including Burgess Cellars, Felton-Empire, and Raymond Vineyards. It is something of a wonder that any Californian fools around with Late Harvest. To an unmatched degree, the wine itself is a result of technique, of managing an unstable microbiological brew with scientific skill. But getting properly moldy grapes is a crapshoot, and a little bit of luck counts for a lot more than scientific wizardry in this game.

A vineyard full of ripe grapes suitable for an old-fashioned dry California Johannisberg Riesling would run something on the order of 21 to 22 degrees Brix as the measure of sugar. Total acid in the grapes would be at least .7 percent, preferably .8. And the fruit would have glossy, gold skin stretched tight over plump berries. A vineyardist can get that. A person with Late Harvest in mind would arrive at that state, then pray for rain or at least a few nights of heavy mist, followed by dry warmth.

"Botrytis spores are omnipresent in California and always have been," says Walter Schug, winemaker at Joseph Phelps. "But . . . conditions for germination must be perfect, and they are not very often." Most of the likely places are "in low-lying areas with higher humidity than average. The problem is, these same conditions are also conducive to the development of other molds." The best hope is for a voluntary infection. The other possibility is to catch a string of warm nights and begin sprinkler irrigation. This latter "is an all-or-nothing proposition," Schug says. "You commit a predetermined acreage to a whim of nature, and the commitment is irreversible. A lack of infection or an infection gone wrong means you do not produce the wine you want."

Either way, the infection must not begin before the grapes reach a sugar level of 17 degrees Brix, or they will sour, for once the infection starts, it spreads and works continuously. "After a vineyard is infected with the mold, the grapes are weakened and indefensible," Schug says.

Larry Langbehn, winemaker at Freemark Abbey, says, "You want the maximum sugar, but you also have to have a botrytis infection without large infections of other molds. You have to have a sense of feel about how long to leave the vineyard versus how much loss you're willing to accept." As dehydration, spoilage, and simple loss diminish the crop, "it becomes very much a trade-off. When you pull the support wires and half the berries fall off, you chicken out. . . . Change in the sugar can be rapid . . . two points a day at some stages. One of our vineyards went from 22 to 34 degrees in six days."

The other aggravation is that field tests do not provide reliable sugar information, so you wait until the grapes are in the winery and crushed. By and large, the producers of sweet Rieslings select bunches to boost the sugar past 30 degrees. By that time the berries are close to mush and no fun to have in the winery.

"Normally," says Freemark Abbey's Langbehn, "the must [freshly crushed fruit] has a certain rigidity . . . like egg whites just before they get stiff. This stuff has no consistency at all. It looks," he says, "like the kind of pea soup a Gold Rush prospector might have made for himself, only browner."

Browning leads to too-dark a color in the wine. The potential for rapid development of vinegar bacteria also requires extra caution. At Chateau St. Jean, winemaker Richard Arrowood pumps caps of carbon dioxide over the grapes for the ride from vineyard to winery and keeps a cloud of gas over them and the wine ever after. But the main problem is getting the soup to move.

"Physical handling at the crusher is very difficult," Langbehn says. "Equipment is all set up for certain weights. This goop is heavier than anything else. Pumps just tear themselves up." At Chateau St. Jean, says Arrowood, "we crush into steel holding tanks. The juice always spends some time in contact with the pulpy mass — you can't call them skins anymore — usually a day to a day and a half. You put that into the press. There is no free-run juice. You press what you can get into tanks, let it settle for a day or two, then centrifuge. After that we inoculate with yeast to start the fermentation." Except that some wineries do not centrifuge, this is fairly standard procedure. "Skin" contact is essential to most winemakers because much of the flavor is derived from it.

Things do not get much easier with fermentation. "You do," says Arrowood, "everything to get up to 10 percent alcohol. Sugar inhibits yeast growth. There's something called the Delle Factor, which states that 2 degrees to 4 degrees of sugar equates to 1 percent of alcohol. Well, if you've got 40 percent sugar that's equal to 10 to 12 percent alcohol, and yeast just has a hard time getting going at that point. I mean, the sugar moves at about two- or three-tenths of a point a week. Fermentations go on into the next year. They finish as late as March . . . Finish! Hah! We just keep pushing until we hit 10 percent, which is the minimum required by a stupid, obsolete state law." (This requirement is in the process of being relaxed.)

Langbehn, at Freemark Abbey, has the same lament. "It's kind of hard to tell when the end of fermentation is. I open the tank and look. When the bubbles look a certain size and form at a certain rate, that's it. We also watch the sugar. If it doesn't change from week to week that's a pretty good sign. We look at the yeasts under a microscope. If they are getting kind of shriveled and sick looking, that's a good sign."

Leo McCloskey, who has begun to make such wines both at Felton-Empire and Smothers in Santa Cruz County, thinks the secret is in the laboratory. "Medical biochemistry is what I do. I'd say that we have five times as much money in the lab [at Felton-Empire] as we do in filters. That's the tipoff. When we filter something, we *know* it should be filtered. We don't guess. This allows us to minimally handle the wine."

Even if minimal, filtering is required, and painful. "Ever try to pump Karo syrup through a brick wall?" Arrowood asks. "Well, that's about it. But you have to have a sterile filtration, otherwise Murphy's Law will give you a second fermentation in the bottle."

It's too soon to know how long California's answers to *auslese* and sweeter styles will last. Eric Wente figures his winery's best efforts — with about 4 percent residual sugar — are at their peak from three to five years, but capable of lasting fifteen for those whose tastes run toward well-aged Riesling. Arrowood at Chateau St. Jean figures his sweetest Rieslings will be in fine fettle for three to seven years with no trouble at all. For lack of experience he will not guess at how long they might go after that. Freemark Abbey's Langbehn gives no guesses. McCloskey figures his first Felton-Empire late harvest wine will go seven years, probably longer.

Food? The consensus is that the slightly sweet models go best with fruit, and the richly sweet ones are best all by themselves. Langbehn dissents. He says brownies are the perfect companion. "Rich, fudgey brownies with lots of butter and nuts — the gooey kind."

## Riesling

Back around 1885, when Johannisberg Riesling was first becoming popular in California, white wine was sweet or dry. Either it fermented all the way or was made so sweet that no yeast could survive the eventual concentrations of sugar and alcohol. There was no halfway. But in these enlightened times, winemakers have the knowledge and the gadgetry to stop a fermentation right where they want to, down to tenths of a percentage point when everything goes just so.

No other grape variety is so well adapted to so many degrees of sweet as Johannisberg or White Riesling. Bone dry, a California Johannisberg has a gentle, soft fruit flavor that does not taste like a pear, but has about the same intensity. With a little residual sugar — and enough acid to offset it — a well-made Johannisberg has the tart-sweet qualities of one of the wild berries — though pinpointing which one is an endless game. With still more sugar, and perhaps a touch of noble mold (*Botrytis cinerea*), it begins to have some of the lush, savory taste of peaches or, more often, apricots.

The original habit of making Johannisberg dry persisted among almost all California winemakers until only a few years ago. If there is a watershed, it probably is 1968, when Lee Stewart produced a memorably rich sweet-tart Johannisberg at the old Souverain Winery, giving many people the idea that coastal California might beat the Germans at their own game.

A small group of traditionalists continues to regard dry Johannisberg as the better bet. Sebastiani is one; another is Christian Brothers. The rest are much smaller cellars: Chappellet, Firestone, Freemark Abbey, Heitz, Stag's Leap Wine Cellar, and Trefethen. Trefethen sums it up: "We use our wines with dinner. We're very fond of dry. We don't drink much sweet."

Dry-wine disciples are in surprising accord on how much sugar should be in the grapes at harvest: Sebastiani and Trefethen both want 22.5 degrees Brix. Larry Langbehn at Freemark Abbey looks for 22 to 22.5 degrees. Joe Heitz of Heitz Cellars, says, "We pick between 21 and 22 degrees. I like wines that are a little sturdy. Pick earlier than that, and you get wines that are thin, acid."

There are two edges to the sword. Trefethen says, "There usually is a threat of rain because it takes the whole season to ripen the bloody things." Freemark Abbey has figured out how to have the best of both worlds. Winemaker Langbehn waits for 22.5 degrees Brix. If the grapes are fat and healthy, he picks. If botrytis shows up by then, the grapes are left to develop as much intensity as possible, and they make Edelwein.

Freemark Abbey's dry Johannisbergs have tasted of oak, but Langbehn says, "It's a vineyard characteristic, not a process. One of our vineyards has characteristics about it that are like wood." Dry Johannisbergs from the winery do spend a brief time in thirteen-hundred gallon oak tanks, but not enough, says Langbehn, to explain the flavor.

"Our aging," says John Trefethen of Trefethen Vineyards, "is entirely in steel. We don't bottle right away. The earliest date would be just ahead of the following crush. Usually we've bottled just after, in January; one wine is about fifteen months old." Heitz takes the shortest view. "We release our Johannisberg in autumn when it's a year old. That's a good time to drink it. Another one or two years is good, but we don't push it too far."

Dry Johannisbergs are versatile. Sebastiani liked his with fish, even more with rice and clams, maybe best of all with meat soups at lunch. "Warm soup on a hot day I like to counterbalance with cool wine." Trefethen elects fish or cold cracked crab. Heitz wants the crab. "If you're lucky, you have some San Francisco French bread, but you don't need that." Freemark Abbey's Langbehn is the odd man out but not unwise: "I like them best on a warm spring afternoon with bright sun and a really nice lady. I drink Johannisberg more by itself than with food. The wine is just visions of warm, grassy hillsides . . . all kinds of really corny, romantic things like that."

If the dry-wine contingent has varying thoughts, the off-dry-to-sweet bloc practices anarchy. Shadings of sweet are extremely subtle from one winery to the next but broad, indeed, from one pole to the other. Some give a hint of wood. Many age only in steel. Some want botrytis in one degree or another, while others view the stuff as a plague. Some want their wines drunk up as soon as they reach the market. Others counsel waiting up to several years. The sweets are much more diverse in character than the drys.

Hank Wetzel at Alexander Valley Vineyards has picked his in the range from 21 to 21.5 degrees Brix, and is "tending toward less ripe grapes. I seem to get a fresher, cleaner style," he says, "and I prefer that. Also, we do not want botrytis. We want to keep the wine as clean and uncomplicated as possible. By uncomplicated, I mean I want Johannisberg Riesling to be as clear as I can make it."

The residual sugar in Wetzel's Johannisbergs tends to stick very close to 1 percent. Eleanor McCrea at Stony Hill would wait for slightly riper grapes, but the general idea is the same; get a prominent varietal character embodied in a brisk, just slightly sweet wine. What is amazing are the different ways they go about it. Wetzel ferments in steel, a shade cooler than many ("Johannisberg can be a problem . . . Fermentations can stick at about 5 degrees residual sugar"), then ages the wine in steel until bottling. "I'm going to experiment with a delayed bottling. We left our 1975 in steel for about five months after getting it cleaned up. That was by accident, but it turned out very well, so I'm going to do it again. We got a distinctive flavor that I would like to repeat."

Stony Hill's Johannisberg, the most direct descendant of the old Souverain, is fermented in wood, then aged in wood. But perish the thought that it taste of wood. "Somebody," says Eleanor McCrea, "once offered to trade us some new barrels for some of our old ones. We didn't. A well-seasoned, healthy barrel is something money can't buy." Well-seasoned is the operative phrase. As tartrate crystals build up, they make the barrel into a very neutral vessel — yet somehow still impart a softness that comes only from wood aging.

Mike Grgich agrees with Wetzel about steel, all steel. "Wood," he says, "would kill the Johannisberg character, which is a very fragile perfume." Grgich likes to have sugars between 1 and 2 degrees, a shade higher than Stony Hill, and even with Wetzel. Where he differs most is on botrytis; Grgich wants some to enrich the varietal character, but not so much it becomes a forceful flavor. Most of Grgich's track record is at Chateau Montelena. His own winery, Grgich Hills, released its first Johannisberg in 1977.

Eric Wente at Wente Bros. prefers a wine that qualifies as Late Harvest, and equates technically with German *spatlese*. Wente likes to pick with the sugar level in the grapes at 27 to 28 degrees Brix, and a tastable concentration of botrytis. At this sugar level the fruit has not broken down as much as it does in another few days, and can be handled more or less normally in a winery. Wente ferments at 45 degrees Fahrenheit, about the same as the others who leave some residual sugar. Also, he uses cooling to stop the fermentation, but he does it a shade earlier — when about 4.5 degrees sugar remains. His alcohol level runs around 11 to 11.5 percent, compared with 12 or a shade more in the Alexander Valley, Stony Hill, and Chateau Montelena wines.

Curiously, the winemakers get together when it comes time to drink the wine. All favor some aging. Wetzel thinks three years begins to hit the mark. So does Wente, with the added thought that people who like really ancient white wine flavors can afford to wait ten, even fifteen years. These gentlemen also favor fruit, either outside a meal or as a dessert, if any food at all has to go along with the wine. Grgich and McCrea like their Johannisbergs with fruit too, but they feel that the wine has enough acidity to be versatile. Either shellfish or chicken in a creamy sauce can be a great accompaniment as well.

# Glossary
# of Varieties

*Here is a brief description of the wines discussed and recommended in the California Living Collection (page 45). The best age at which to drink the wine follows each description.*

BARBERA    An Italian grape variety, it produces a fruity wine with substantial acidity that is the wine of choice with garlicky pasta dishes. Best with moderate age, four to six years.

BURGUNDY    In California, this can mean any red wine blend, often a little on the sweet side, although the better ones are dry and elegant. It is not to be confused with French Burgundy. California Burgundies are usually ready to drink when sold, although the dry ones improve with some age.

CABERNET SAUVIGNON    To many, the king of California varietals, the grape makes a red wine of distinctive character, variously referred to as herbaceous, olivelike, minty, or eucalyptus. The wines are often aged for one to three years in small oak casks; this mellows the wine and adds wood and vanilla aromas and flavors for complexity. The best of these are worthy of long and careful aging in the bottle, and few are ready to drink before four years after the vintage date. Often ten to fifteen years' age is extremely beneficial to the wine's elegance and complexity.

CARIGNANE    This is the second most widely planted red grape variety in California. It makes a wine that is the backbone of most generic reds, with neutral aromas and flavors. Best drunk young.

CHABLIS    The white wine counterpart of Burgundy, above, not to be confused with French Chablis. In restaurants, the word has become synonymous with generic white wine of any kind. Drink young.

CHAMPAGNE    The best are made in the traditional Champagne method, and they have "Fermented in This Bottle" printed on the label. Bulk-process sparkling wines can represent good value, however. Ready to drink when purchased.

CHARBONO    An Italian grape with a distinctive flowery fruitiness and fuller body than Barbera, which the wines resemble. Only a few are made, and they are best with four to six years' age.

CHARDONNAY    The queen of the white grapes, this is the grape that produces some of the finest white wines in the world. Often the wines are aged in oak, picking up distinctive wood and vanilla aromas and flavors for complexity. The grape's natural aroma is said to remind one of green apples. Best with three to five years' age.

CHENIN BLANC    At its best, a lovely, fruity, charming wine, often made with some residual sweetness for sipping between meals rather than matching with food. It is the second most widely planted white grape in California, and much of it goes into anonymous white blends. Drink it young.

CHIANTI    A red wine blend, usually on the tart side, but sometimes noticeably sweet, not to be confused with the Italian wine of the same name. Ready to drink when purchased.

EMERALD RIESLING    A cross between White Riesling and a little-known grape called Muscadelle de Bordelais, this makes light wines with a kind of flowery fruitiness that are usually a little bit sweet. Drink it young.

FOLLE BLANCHE    Only one winery makes a wine from this grape — a tart, fruity, not especially distinctive light wine. Drink it young.

FRENCH COLOMBARD    The most widely planted white wine grape in California, it is the backbone of white wine blends and bulk-process sparkling wines because of its remarkable ability to retain acidity as it ripens. The wines are fruity, lighter than Chenin Blanc, not distinctive but often pleasant. Drink them young.

FUMÉ BLANC    A proprietary name often used to identify Sauvignon Blanc wines. *Fumé* means "smoke" in French, and the wines are thought to have a smoky character. See Sauvignon Blanc below.

GAMAY BEAUJOLAIS    Once thought to be the grape that grows in Beaujolais, France, it is now known to be a clone of Pinot Noir. The wines tend to be made in a light, fruity style, often developing a spicy character. Ready to drink when sold.

GEWURZTRAMINER    *Gewürz* means "spicy" in German, and this grape does make wines that can be called spicy, although the word flowery is often applied to the lighter versions. Some of the wines are made dry, but most of the better ones have some residual sweetness. It usually takes one to two years from the vintage date for it to develop its full character.

GREEN HUNGARIAN    The name is much more colorful than the wine, which tends to be neutral, light, and pleasant. Drink it young.

GRENACHE ROSÉ    Grenache is a red grape that is used almost exclusively to make rosés because that seems to be the best way to develop its full fruitiness. Grenache rosés tend to be less sweet than other California generic rosés.

GRIGNOLINO    An Italian grape that, like the Barbera and Charbono above, tends to make tart wine, only less fruity and more austere. Best with three to five years' age.

JOHANNISBERG RIESLING    The predominant name for what is properly called White Riesling. The wine is almost always at least a little bit sweet, in which case it has a distinctive honeysuckle aroma, but Late-Harvest types made from overripe grapes, as they get sweeter, develop honey-like, peach, or apricot aromas. Some of the greatest wines ever made in California were made from this grape. The light wines usually take one to one and a half years from the vintage date to develop their full character, but don't wait too long to drink them. Freshness is a part of the charm.

MERLOT    This grape, a native of Bordeaux (primarily St. Emilion), makes wines that are similar in some respects to Cabernet Sauvignon but not usually as intense or long-lived. The distinctive aroma is often likened to green olives, and the wines tend to be on the medium to light side. They are best with three to five years' age.

PETITE SIRAH    Several grapes have been working under this name, but the bulk of them seem to be the Duriff, a little-known European variety. The wines are often tannic but still fruity with a distinct black-pepper spiciness. Best with lots of age, eight to ten years if possible.

PINOT BLANC    A white wine grape that can make wines of impressive richness and body; at their best, better than some Chardonnays. Allow one and a half to two years to develop its full character.

PINOT CHARDONNAY    Once it was thought that Chardonnay was a member of the Pinot family, botanically speaking. It is not, but old habits die hard. Don't hold it against the wine that it may be misnamed. (See Chardonnay.)

PINOT NOIR    The enfant terrible of California wine, this notoriously difficult grape has, on a remarkable number of occasions, made spectacularly fruity and complex wines. But it also often slips into mediocrity. California Pinot Noirs are better than their reputation, often excellent wines. Give them three to six years from the vintage date to develop in the bottle.

PINOT ST. GEORGE    A generally fruity but not very distinctive red wine is made from this Burgundian grape. Best at three to five years.

SAUVIGNON BLANC    The coming grape variety in California, it makes white wines of distinctive character that are less expensive than Chardonnay because they don't need much, if any, oak aging. The aromas and flavors are often likened to herbs or cut grass. A few sweet wines have been made from this varietal; these have an intensely weedy character that some like, others don't.

WHITE RIESLING    The proper name of the king of the Germanic grapes, described above as Johannisberg Riesling. A few wineries are using the proper name, but it is taking them longer to catch on to this one than to Chardonnay.

ZINFANDEL    The most widely planted wine grape in California, whose origin has been the subject of speculation for decades, although the best evidence is that it is the Italian Primitivo. The distinctive character of the wines suggest the aroma and flavors of crushed berries, in some regions cherries. Depending on how and where the grape is grown, it can make wines of light body and fruity charm, medium body and intense fruit, or heavy body and high tannin, the latter producing a roughness on the palate that takes years of aging to mellow. You will also find rosés and "white" wines made from Zinfandel, the latter actually a sort of bronze color. Drink the light ones early, the heavier ones in four to ten years, depending on the nature of the wine.

# The
# California Living
# Wine Collection

# Introduction

The region, county, or valley designation on a bottle of wine tells you something about its contents, just as a particular address — say in Beverly Hills — can tell you something about a house. A good part of the character of a wine is defined by where the grapes were grown, and this location is stated on the label with the appellation. If the grapes come from a specific area, the wine is entitled to carry the appellation of that area. If the wine is made from grapes grown in several areas, the wine usually carries a "California" appellation.

The geographical appellation, which appears on the label above the type of wine, can be a state, county, or viticultural area. To carry a county appellation such as Napa, Sonoma, or Monterey, a minimum of 75 percent of the grapes must come from that county. For a viticultural area such as Alexander Valley, Carneros Region, or North Coast, the minimum is 85 percent.

In the fall of 1978, the federal regulations for appellations of origin were revised, scheduled to go into full effect January 1, 1983. A lawsuit filed in 1979 by three wine consumers challenged these regulations, among others. A Washington, D.C., federal judge sent the regulations back to the Bureau of Alcohol, Tobacco and Firearms in November, 1979, for rewriting. At publication time, the case was on appeal.

The government plans to hold hearings to define such viticultural areas before 1983. The federal court decision of 1979 mandates only that the regulations require explanations on the label of these minimum percentages when the actual percentages run less than 100 percent.

The following list of selected California wines was chosen specifically to allow comparison of the range of wines made in the various regions. The wines are categorized by appellation, their place of origin — not the location of the winery. You might want to do a tasting of several wines, all of the same type but from different regions. A comparative tasting of Zinfandels might include those from Sonoma, Napa, Amador, Santa Cruz, Monterey, San Luis Obispo, Santa Barbara, and San Joaquin (probably labeled "California" and made by a Central Valley producer). The Sonoma wine might have a taste of flowery fruitiness, while the Napa wine is less generous or full, but more complex. The Amador wine might be described as intensely aromatic and alcoholic, while the Santa Cruz wine is grapey, and perhaps a little coarse. The blackberry flavor characteristic of this grape variety is caught in the Monterey wine, while the San Luis Obispo sample may taste more like cherries. Santa Barbara might be rich and full-bodied, with the San Joaquin tasting light and more delicate.

And this is only the Zinfandel. Differences among the regions of California show up just as dramatically in Cabernet Sauvignon, Sauvignon Blanc, Chardonnay, White Riesling, and Gewurztraminer. Each of these grape varieties has considerable character of its own. Grapes with less varietal identity will probably vary less from region to region.

Then, too, regional character is only one among many variables that define the character of the grapes. The age of the vineyard, the type of pruning, how the vine is trained to the trellises, whether the vineyard is irrigated or dry-farmed, all these and more affect the aroma and flavor of the grapes — the grapes now, not the wine. Once the winemaker gets them, he or she guides the fermentation process, cellar treatment, and aging, and all these also shape the final character of the wine. A particular winemaker's approach explains why all the Zinfandels in the Napa Valley don't taste alike, any more than all the Rieslings from the Rheingau in Germany do. Though the processes of making wine involve many technical details, winemaking itself is understandably referred to as an art.

In spite of all these variables wine drinkers do recognize the appellation — the birthplace of the grape — as one of the key factors. A well-earned reputation for quality goes along with such growing regions in California as Napa Valley, Alexander Valley, Dry Creek Valley, Sonoma Valley, Mendocino County, and the Carneros district. Some relatively new regions are currently earning their stripes — Monterey County, Amador County, San Luis Obispo County (both Paso Robles and Edna valleys), and Santa Barbara County (both Santa Maria and Santa Ynez valleys). It is possible that the individual counties of the Central Valley may someday become noted, too, as more and more excellent wines are made from grapes grown there.

In the list that follows, the winegrowing districts of California are divided into five regions. Region A on the map comprises Napa and Solano Counties. Region B is Sonoma, Mendocino, Lake, Marin, and Humboldt counties. Region C is what has come to be known as the Central Coast, the counties stretching south of San Francisco to Santa Barbara. Region D is the San Joaquin Valley, the great central farming region stretching from Redding in the north to the Tehachapis in the south. Region E is Southern California, from the Tehachapis down to the Mexican border.

Regions A, B, and C share a common climatic influence — the cooling fogs of the Pacific Ocean. The temperature ranges of the coastal valleys stretching from Mendocino to Santa Barbara are essentially the same. The differences between these regions are caused by soil types, elevation, and distance from the ocean (in the case of Napa, from San Pablo Bay) rather than latitude. Some of the coolest regions are to the south, some of the warmest to the north. Most of Mendocino County's vineyards get more heat than those of Monterey or Santa Barbara.

Napa and Sonoma counties (Regions A and B) have histories of wine-growing that date back to shortly after the Gold Rush. Mendocino County (Region B) is a little more recent, but winegrowing there still predates the beginning of this century. Vineyards were common in San Luis Obispo County (Region C) around Paso Robles and Templeton near the turn of the century, and some of the finest Zinfandels in the state are reputed to have been made there. The first vineyards in Monterey County were planted after Prohibition, and the burst of planting there in the late 1960s and early 1970s propelled Monterey into the number one spot in total vineyard acreage of all the coastal counties. The relative newcomers are in Santa Barbara County (still Region C).

Scientific advances in viticulture opened up the Central Valley for quality wine production. Although grapes have been grown there since the mid-nineteenth century, only since the early 1960s, with the advances in winemaking technology, have uniformly good wines been produced there — and at remarkably reasonable prices. The Central Valley is primarily responsible for the worldwide reputation of California jug wines as the finest of the world's modestly priced wines.

Southern California (Region E) actually has the longest viticultural history; this is where the Mission fathers planted the first wine grapes in California. A thriving winemaking industry in the late nineteenth century never recovered from Prohibition, but there are a few pockets of cool valleys in Riverside and San Diego counties producing some exciting wines today.

In the listings that follow, the name of the winery is followed by the name of the county in which the grapes were grown for that particular wine. In some cases, the label reflects an even narrower appellation, such as a particular valley or vineyard. Wines that carry a wider appellation, such as "North Coast" or "California," are listed according to the location of the winery.

Within each category, the wines are listed according to type as noted on the label. Therefore, you will find separate listings for Fumé Blanc and Sauvignon Blanc, although they are the same grape variety. White Riesling and Johannisberg Riesling — also the same grape — are listed separately too.

The prices listed are the suggested retail prices for a 750-milliliter bottle (called a fifth or ¾ liter) and were obtained from records of the State Alcoholic Beverage Control Board or the winery and are presumed to be accurate as of February, 1980. These prices are not necessarily those you will find at your local wine shop or supermarket, as discount stores may sell these wines at lower prices, and some specialty shops may mark highly prized bottles somewhat higher.

# Listing
# by Region

## Region A
## Napa and Solano Counties

BARBERA

Louis Martini, California, $3.45.

BURGUNDY

Beringer, North Coast, $2.50.

CABERNET SAUVIGNON

Beaulieu, Napa, $6.00.
Beaulieu Private Reserve, Napa, $12.00.
Burgess, Napa, $8.75.
Carneros Creek, Napa, $7.75.
Caymus, Napa, $10.00.
Chappellet, Napa, $10.00.
Charles Krug, Napa, $5.50.
Chateau Chevalier, Napa, $8.75.
Chateau Montelena, Napa, $9.00.

Christian Brothers Vintage, Napa, $6.00.
Clos du Val, Napa, $9.00.
Cuvaison, Napa, $7.50.
Franciscan, Napa, $6.49.
Freemark Abbey, (Bosche Vineyard) Napa, $8.50.
Louis Martini Regular Bottling, Napa, $4.50.
Louis Martini Private Reserve, Napa, $5.50.
Mayacamas, Napa, $12.00.
Mt. Veeder, Napa, $10.00.
Ridge (York Creek), Napa, $12.00.
Robert Mondavi Regular Bottling, Napa, $8.00.
Robert Mondavi Private Reserve, Napa, $20.00.
Rutherford Hill, Napa, $5.00.
Spring Mountain, Napa, $8.50.

Stag's Leap Wine Cellars, Napa, $10.00.
Sterling Private Reserve, Napa, $20.00.
Stonegate, Napa, $8.50.

CHABLIS

Charles Krug, California, $3.00.
Louis Martini, California, $2.90.

CHAMPAGNE

Beaulieu Champagne de Chardonnay, Napa, $9.92.
Domaine Chandon Napa Valley Blanc de Noir, Napa, $10.40.
Domaine Chandon Napa Valley Brut, Napa, $10.40.
Hanns Kornell Sehr Trocken, California, $11.50.
Schramsberg Blanc de Blanc, Napa, $9.50.
Schramsberg Cuvée de Gamay, Napa, $8.85.

CHARBONO

Inglenook, Napa, $5.50.

CHARDONNAY

Beringer, Napa, $6.50.
Burgess, Napa, $9.75.
Chappellet, Napa, $10.00.
Chateau Montelena, Napa, $10.00.
Christian Brothers, Napa, $4.75.
Cuvaison, Napa, $8.00.
Freemark Abbey, Napa, $9.75.
Heitz, Napa, $15.00.
Joseph Phelps, Napa, $8.75.
Mayacamas, Napa, $9.00.
Mt. Veeder, Napa, $18.00.
Robert Mondavi, Napa, $10.00.
Spring Mountain, Napa, $8.50.
Sterling, Napa, $10.00.
Stonegate, Napa, $8.00.

Stony Hill, Napa, $9.00.
Trefethen, Napa, $7 50.
Villa Mt. Eden, Napa, $10.00

CHENIN BLANC

Chappellet, Napa, $6.00.
Charles Krug, Napa, $4.00.
Franciscan, Napa, $4.49.
Grand Cru, Yolo, $4.75.
Robert Mondavi, Napa, $4.75.

CHIANTI

Louis Martini, California, $2.90.

FOLLE BLANCHE

Louis Martini, Napa, $4.25.

FRENCH COLOMBARD

Gavilan, Napa, $3.99.
Robert Pecota, Napa, $4.00.

FUMÉ BLANC

Christian Brothers, Napa, $4.60.
Robert Mondavi, Napa, $6.75.

GAMAY BEAUJOLAIS

Charles Krug, Napa, $4.00.
Robert Pecota, Napa, (Nouveau), $4.25.
Stag's Leap Wine Cellars, Napa, $3.50.

GEWURZTRAMINER

Charles Krug, Napa, $5.00.
Christian Brothers, Napa, $6.00.
Joseph Phelps, Napa, $4.75.
Rutherford Hill, Napa, $4.50.
Villa Mt. Eden, Napa, $5.00.

GRIGNOLINO

Beringer, Napa, $3.75.
Heitz, Napa, $5.00.

JOHANNISBERG RIESLING

Beaulieu, (Beauclair) Napa, $5.00.
Beringer, Napa, $5.50.
Burgess, (Winery Lake) Napa, $8.50.
Chappellet, Napa, $6.00.
Chateau Montelena, North Coast, $5.50.
Freemark Abbey, Napa, $4.50.
Freemark Abbey Sweet Select, $9.00.
Grgich Hills, Napa, $6.50.
Heitz, Napa, $5.50.
Joseph Phelps, Napa, $5.00.
Long Vineyard, Botrytised, Napa, $9.00.
Rutherford Hill, Napa, $4.50.
Rutherford Vintners, Napa, $6.00.
Trefethen, Napa, $6.00.

MERLOT

Stag's Leap Wine Cellars, Napa, $9.00.
Sterling, Napa, $8.00.

MUSCAT BLANC

Inglenook, Napa Valley, $4.00.

PETITE SIRAH

Carneros Creek, Napa, $6.50.
Freemark Abbey, (York Creek) Napa, $6.00.
Stonegate, Napa, $6.50.

PINOT BLANC

Inglenook, Napa, $4.50.

PINOT NOIR

Beaulieu, Napa, $4.50.
Beringer, Napa, $5.00.
Carneros Creek, Napa, $10.00.
Caymus, Napa, $7.00.
Freemark Abbey, Napa, $6.00.

Raymond, Napa, $6.50.
Robert Mondavi, Napa, $6.50.
Rutherford Hill, Napa, $4.50.
Sterling, Napa, $6.00.

PINOT NOIR (NOUVEAU)

Rutherford Hill, Napa, $4.00.

PINOT ST. GEORGE

Christian Brothers, Napa, $6.00.

SAUVIGNON BLANC

Joseph Phelps, Napa, $6.50.
Pope Valley, Napa, $4.50.
Sterling, Napa, $6.00.
Stonegate, Napa, $6.50.

SYRAH

Joseph Phelps, Napa, $6.00.

WHITE RIESLING

Franciscan, Napa, $5.99.
Stony Hill, Napa, $7.50.
Trefethen, Napa, $3.95.

ZINFANDEL

Chateau Montelena, North Coast, $6.00.
Christian Brothers, Napa, $3.50.
Clos du Val, Napa, $7.50.
Cuvaison, Napa, $4.50.
Louis Martini, California, $4.00.
Raymond, Napa, $5.50.
Sterling, Napa, $6.00.

# Region B
## Sonoma and Mendocino Counties

BARBERA

Sebastiani, North Coast, $4.25.

BURGUNDY

Hacienda, Sonoma, $3.00.

Kenwood, Sonoma, $3.50.
Sebastiani, North Coast, $3.00.

CABERNET SAUVIGNON

Alexander Valley, Sonoma, $5.50.
Buena Vista Cask Reserve, Sonoma, $8.00.
Chateau St. Jean, Sonoma, $10.00.
Edmeades, Mendocino, $4.50.
Fetzer (Estate Bottled), Mendocino, $6.50.
Foppiano, Sonoma, $5.50.
Kenwood, Sonoma, $8.50.
Parducci, Mendocino, $5.50.
Pedroncelli, Sonoma, $4.00.
Simi, Sonoma, $6.00.
Sonoma Vineyards, (Alexander's Crown) Sonoma, $10.00.
Souverain, North Coast, $4.95.

CARIGNANE

Fetzer, Mendocino, $2.75.
Parducci, Mendocino, $3.50.
Simi, Sonoma, $2.95.

CHABLIS

Buena Vista, North Coast, $3.75.

CHAMPAGNE

Chateau St. Jean Blanc de Noir, Sonoma, $9.50.
Korbel Brut, California, $7.00.

CHARBONO

Souverain, North Coast, $4.00.

CHARDONNAY

Alexander Valley, Sonoma, $7.50.
Buena Vista, (Estate Bottled) Sonoma, $8.00.
Chateau St. Jean, (Robert Young Vineyard) Sonoma, $10.00.
Davis Bynum, Sonoma, $7.50.

Dehlinger, Sonoma, $7.50.
Dry Creek, Sonoma, $8.00.
Edmeades, Mendocino, $6.50.
Gundlach-Bundschu, Sonoma, $10.00.
Hanzell, Sonoma, $10.00.
Husch, Mendocino, $7.50.
Joseph Swan, Sonoma, $10.00.
Korbel, Sonoma, $5.25.
Parducci, Mendocino, $6.00.
River Oaks, Sonoma, $5.49.
Simi, Sonoma, $7.00.
Sonoma Vineyards, (River West) Sonoma, $7.25.
Veedercrest, Sonoma, $9.50.

CHENIN BLANC

Alexander Valley, Sonoma, $5.00.
Cambiaso, Sonoma, $4.00.
Grand Cru, Yolo, $4.75.
Johnson's Alexander Valley, Sonoma, $3.75.
Kenwood, Sonoma, $4.75.
Landmark, Sonoma, $4.50.
Parducci, Mendocino, $4.00.
Sonoma Vineyards, Sonoma, $3.90.

FRENCH COLOMBARD

Mark West, Sonoma, $3.75.
Sonoma Vineyards, Sonoma, $3.11.
Souverain, North Coast, $3.00.

FUMÉ BLANC

Chateau St. Jean, Sonoma, $6.50.
Dry Creek, Sonoma, $6.00.
Souverain, North Coast, $5.00.

GAMAY

Mill Creek, Sonoma, $3.75.
Pedroncelli, Sonoma, $3.00.
Trentadue, Sonoma, $2.75.

GAMAY BEAUJOLAIS

Parducci, Mendocino, $3.50.

GEWURZTRAMINER

Buena Vista, Sonoma, $5.99.
Chateau St. Jean, Sonoma, $6.75.
Clos du Bois, Sonoma, $5.50.
Edmeades, Mendocino, $5.95.
Geyser Peak, Sonoma, $5.25.
Grand Cru, (Garden Creek Ranch)
  Sonoma, $7.50.
Hacienda, Sonoma, $6.00.
Hop Kiln, Sonoma, $5.50.
Husch, Mendocino, $6.00.
Pedroncelli, Sonoma, $4.37.

GREEN HUNGARIAN

Buena Vista, Sonoma, $4.25.
Sebastiani, North Coast, $3.75.

GRENACHE ROSÉ

Sonoma Vineyards, Sonoma,
  $3.90.

JOHANNISBERG RIESLING

Alexander Valley, Sonoma, $4.25.
Chateau St. Jean, (Belle Terre
  Vineyard, Selected Late Har-
  vest) Sonoma, $10.00.
Clos du Bois, Sonoma, $5.50.
Geyser Peak, Sonoma, $5.00.
Landmark, Sonoma, $5.00.
Simi, Sonoma, $6.00.
Sonoma Vineyards, (LeBaron)
  Sonoma, $9.75.
Souverain, North Coast, $4.49.

LATE-HARVEST RIESLING

Buena Vista, Sonoma, $8.00.
Chateau St. Jean, (Individual Dry
  Bunch Selected, Belle Terre
  Vineyard) Sonoma, $25.00
  (half-bottle).
Hacienda, Sonoma, $9.00.

MERLOT

Gundlach-Bundschu, Sonoma,
  $6.00.

PETITE SIRAH

Field Stone, Sonoma, $8.50.
Foppiano, Sonoma, $4.00.
Hop Kiln, Sonoma, $8.00.
Kenwood, Sonoma, $4.50.
Parducci, Mendocino, $4.50.
Sonoma Vineyards, Sonoma,
  $4.40.
Souverain, North Coast, $4.49.

PINOT BLANC

Chateau St. Jean, Sonoma, $5.00.
Fetzer, Mendocino, $6.00.

PINOT NOIR

Buena Vista, Sonoma, $5.00.
Davis Bynum, Sonoma, $5.50.
Grand Cru, Sonoma, $5.00.
Gundlach-Bundschu, Sonoma,
  $7.00.
Hanzell, Sonoma, $10.00.
Husch, Mendocino, $7.50.
Joseph Swan, Sonoma, $6.50.
J. W. Morris, Sonoma, $6.00.
Parducci, Mendocino, $5.00.
Sonoma Vineyards, (Estate Bot-
  tled) Sonoma, $6.50.
Souverain, North Coast, $4.25.

SAUVIGNON BLANC

Chateau St. Jean, (Pat Paulsen
  Vineyard) Sonoma, $7.50.
Dry Creek, Sonoma, $6.50.
Foppiano, Sonoma Fumé, Sonoma,
  $6.00.
Preston, Sonoma, $6.50.

ZINFANDEL

Buena Vista, Sonoma, $4.25.
Burgess, Sonoma, $6.50.

Cuvaison, Napa, $4.50.
Dehlinger, Sonoma, $5.50.
Dry Creek, Sonoma, $5.25.
Fetzer, Mendocino, $5.50.
Foppiano, Sonoma, $4.00.
Grand Cru, Sonoma, $3.95.
Hop Kiln, Sonoma, $4.50.
Johnson's Alexander Valley, Sonoma, $6.50.
Joseph Swan, Sonoma, $7.50.
Kenwood, Sonoma, $5.50.
Lytton Springs, Sonoma, $6.50.
Parducci, Mendocino, $3.50.
Preston, Sonoma, $5.50.
Ridge, (York Creek) Sonoma, $6.50.
Sebastiani, North Coast, $3.75.
Souverain, Sonoma, $3.50.

# Region C
## Central Coast

### BARBERA
Pedrizzetti, Santa Clara, $2.75.

### BURGUNDY
Paul Masson, California, $2.43.
Pedrizzetti, Santa Clara, $1.99.

### CABERNET SAUVIGNON
Almaden, Monterey, $4.00.
Charles LeFranc, Monterey, $4.00.
Concannon, Alameda, $9.00.
David Bruce, Santa Cruz, $7.50.
Estrella River, San Luis Obispo, $7.00.
Firestone, Santa Barbara, $6.50.
Fortino, Santa Clara, $5.50.
Hoffman Mountain Ranch, San Luis Obispo, $10.00.
Mirassou Harvest Selection, Monterey, $6.50.

Monterey Peninsula, Monterey, $4.75.
Ridge, (Monte Bello) Santa Clara, $10.00.
Sherrill Cellars, (Gilroy) Santa Clara, $6.00.
Zaca Mesa, Santa Barbara, $6.50.

### CHABLIS
Paul Masson, California, $2.49.
San Martin, California, $2.10.
Wente, California, $2.75.

### CHAMPAGNE
Almaden Blanc de Blanc, California, $7.25.

### CHARBONO
Fortino, Santa Clara, $4.50.

### CHARDONNAY
Barengo, Santa Barbara, $5.25.
Chalone, Monterey, $5.75.
David Bruce, Santa Cruz, $4.50.
Estrella River, San Luis Obispo, $7.50.
Firestone, Santa Barbara, $7.50.
Hoffman Mountain Ranch, (Edna Valley), San Luis Obispo, $8.50.
Jekel, Monterey, $7.00.
Mirassou Harvest Selection, Monterey, $6.50.
Z-D, Santa Barbara, $10.00.

### CHENIN BLANC
Bargetto, Santa Cruz, $1.99.
Hoffman Mountain Ranch, San Luis Obispo, $4.50.
J. Lohr, Monterey, $3.50.
Novitiate, Santa Clara, $3.25.

### GAMAY
J. Lohr, Monterey, $3.50.

GAMAY BEAUJOLAIS

Monterey Vineyard, Monterey, $4.00.
Weibel, Alameda, $3.50.

GEWURZTRAMINER

Almaden, Monterey, $3.75.
Cresta Blanca, San Luis Obispo, $3.50.
Firestone, Santa Barbara, $5.00.
Mirassou, Santa Clara, $4.75.
Monterey Vineyard, Monterey, $4.75.
Z-D, Santa Barbara, $5.00.

GREEN HUNGARIAN

Weibel, Alameda, $5.85.

GRENACHE ROSÉ

Almaden, San Benito, $1.80.

GREY RIESLING

Wente, Alameda, $4.00.

JOHANNISBERG RIESLING

Concannon, Alameda, $4.75.
Felton-Empire, (Santa Maria) San Luis Obispo, $8.00.
Firestone (1976), Santa Barbara, $5.00.
Hoffman Mountain Ranch, San Luis Obispo, $5.50.
Jekel, Monterey, $5.00.
Mirassou, Monterey, $4.25.
Monterey Vineyard,˙ Monterey, $2.95.
Wente, Monterey, $3.75.
Zaca Mesa, Santa Barbara, $3.95.

LE BLANC DE BLANC

Wente, Monterey, $3.25.

MERLOT

Z-D, San Luis Obispo, $9.00.

MONTEREY RIESLING

Mirassou, Monterey, $3.95.

MUSCAT BLANC

Concannon, Alameda, $4.50.

MUSCAT CANELLI

Estrella River, San Luis Obispo, $5.50.

PETITE ROSÉ

Mirassou, Monterey, $3.25.

PETITE SIRAH

Ahlgren, Monterey, $6.00.
Concannon, California, $4.00.
Mirassou, Monterey, $4.19.
Pedrizzetti, San Luis Obispo, $3.75.
San Martin, Monterey, $4.00.

PINOT BLANC

Chalone, Monterey, $5.00.
J. Lohr, Monterey, $4.50.
Roudon-Smith, Monterey, $6.50
Wente, Monterey, $4.50.

PINOT NOIR

Chalone, Monterey, $5.00.
David Bruce, Santa Cruz, $5.50.
Hoffman Mountain Ranch, San Luis Obispo, $15.00.
J. Lohr, Monterey, $6.00.
Mirassou, Monterey, $5.00.
Monterey Vineyard, Monterey, $6.00.
Novitiate, Santa Clara, $3.75.
San Martin, Monterey, $4.50.

RKATSITELI

Concannon, Livermore, $4.50.

SAUVIGNON BLANC

Concannon, Alameda, $5.25.

Estrella River, San Luis Obispo, $4.75.

Monterey Vineyard, Monterey, $10.00.

Santa Ynez Valley, Santa Barbara, $6.00.

THOMPSON SEEDLESS

Thomas Kruse "Chutzpah," $4.00.

WHITE BURGUNDY

Mirassou, Monterey, $4.99.

WHITE RIESLING

Z-D, Santa Barbara, $5.50.

ZINFANDEL

Bargetto, Santa Cruz, $1.79.
Calera, California, $3.75.
Calera Zin, San Luis Obisbo, $6.00.
David Bruce, Santa Cruz, $4.50.
Enz, San Benito, $4.00.
Monterey Vineyard December Harvest, Monterey, $3.95.
Ridge, (Paso Robles) San Luis Obispo, $5.00.
Roudon-Smith, Santa Cruz, $5.00.
San Martin, Monterey, $3.50.
Thomas Kruse, Santa Clara, $4.50.
Zaca Mesa, Santa Barbara, $4.50.

# Region D
## The Central Valley

BARBERA

Angelo Papagni, Madera, $3.25.
Giumarra, California, $1.39.
Montevina, Amador, $5.00.
J. W. Morris, Amador, $4.00.

CABERNET SAUVIGNON

Colony, California, $1.89.
Growers, California, $1.49.
Montevina, Amador, $5.00.
Rancho Yerba Buena, Madera, $3.50.
Shenandoah, Amador, $6.50.

CHABLIS

Guasti, $2.00.
M. LaMont, California, $1.79.

CHABLIS BLANC

Gallo, California, $1.87.

CHARDONNAY

Angelo Papagni, Madera, $6.00.

CHENIN BLANC

Angelo Papagni Sparkling Chenin Blanc, Madera, $5.50.

EMERALD RIESLING

Angelo Papagni Late Harvest, Madera, $6.50.

FRENCH COLOMBARD

Ambassador, California, $1.89.
Gallo, California, $1.99.
Giumarra, California, $1.53.
Guasti, California, $1.99.
Guild, California, $1.99.
M. LaMont, California, $1.89.

GEWURZTRAMINER

Gallo, California, $3.19.
M. LaMont, California, $1.89.

JOHANNISBERG RIESLING

Gallo, California, $2.79.

SAUVIGNON BLANC

Gallo, California, $2.39.

ZINFANDEL

Franzia, California, $1.69.
M. LaMont, California, $1.89.
Montevina Special Selection, Amador, $6.00.
Shenandoah, Amador, $4.75.

# Region E
## Southern California

CHARDONNAY

Franciscan, (Temecula) Riverside, $7.49.

CHENIN BLANC

Callaway, Riverside, $4.75.
San Pasqual, San Diego, $4.50.

GAMAY

San Pasqual, San Diego, $4.00.

PETITE SIRAH

Assumption Abbey, Riverside, $4.00.
Callaway, Riverside, $6.75.

SAUVIGNON BLANC

San Pasqual, San Diego, $4.75.

ZINFANDEL

Callaway, Riverside, $5.50.

## Fortified Wines

Fortified wines are made by adding brandy or high-proof neutral spirits to newly fermented wine, for dry wines, or to fermenting wine to stop the fermentation, for sweet wines, such as ports. By definition, these wines have no regional character to speak of, as the character comes from the process.

ANGELICA

Assumption Abbey, $3.00.
Heitz Cellar Treasure, $4.00.
Novitiate, $2.75.

DRY SHERRIES

Angelo Papagni Finest Hour, $6.50.
Christian Brothers Cocktail, $2.50.
Conti-Royale Cocktail Dry, $2.00.
Guasti Pale Dry, $3.59.
Llords and Elwood Gr-r-reat Day, $4.25.
San Martin Dry, $2.79.
Sebastiani Areas Dry, $5.50.

MUSCAT

Novitiate Black Muscat, $4.95.
Novitiate Muscat Frontignan, $3.75.

RUBY PORT

Llords and Elwood Ancient Proverb, $4.25.
J. W. Morris Founder's Port, $5.50.
J. W. Morris Vintage Port, $6.75.
Paul Masson Souzao, $4.99.
Quady, $6.50.

SWEET SHERRIES

Cresta Blanca Triple Cream, $3.50.
Gallo Livingston Cream, $1.89.
San Martin Cream, $2.79.
Sebastiani Amore Cream, $5.50.
Weibel Solera Flor California Amber, $3.00.

TINTA PORT

Conti-Royale Tinta Madeira, $3.00.
Ficklin, $5.00.
Novitiate Tinta Port, $3.00.
Sonoma Vineyards Tawny Port, $3.00.

# Listing
# by Variety

In the listing that follows, the California Living Wine List is organized according to the type or variety of wine. Under each major heading, such as Cabernet Sauvignon, there are regional designations so that you can pick out three Cabernets from one region or three from three different regions, as you wish. Many of the wine types are also the names of grape varieties — Barbera, Chardonnay, Gamay Beaujolais, Merlot, Chenin Blanc, Pinot Noir, Johannisberg Riesling, Sauvignon Blanc, and Zinfandel. Some are generic, denoting a general type of wine, such as Chablis and Burgundy, which derive their names from winegrowing regions in France; others use proprietary names, such as Petite Rosé and Monterey Riesling, which are coined by the winery.

Remember that these are the suggested retail prices as of February, 1980. They are likely to change with an individual store's pricing policy, if not with the vagaries of our economy.

# Barbera

REGION A

Louis Martini, California, $3.45.

REGION B

Sebastiani, North Coast, $4.25.

REGION C

Pedrizzetti, Santa Clara, $2.75.

REGION D

Angelo Papagni, Madera, $3.25.
Giumarra, California, $1.39.
J. W. Morris, Amador, $4.00.

# Black Muscat

REGION C

Novitiate, Santa Clara, $4.95.

# Burgundy

REGION A

Beringer, North Coast, $2.50.

REGION B

Hacienda, Sonoma, $3.00.
Kenwood, Sonoma, $3.50.
Sebastiani, North Coast, $3.00.

REGION C

Paul Masson, California, $2.43.
Pedrizzetti, Santa Clara, $1.99.

# Cabernet Sauvignon

REGION A

Beaulieu, Napa, $6.00.
Beaulieu Private Reserve, Napa,
 $12.00.

Burgess, Napa, $8.75.
Carneros Creek, Napa, $7.75.
Caymus, Napa, $10.00.
Charles Krug, Napa, $5.50.
Chateau Chevalier, Napa, $8.75.
Chateau Montelena, Napa, $9.00.
Christian Brothers Vintage,
 Napa, $6.00.
Clos du Val, Napa, $9.00.
Cuvaison, Napa, $7.50.
Franciscan, Napa, $6.49.
Freemark Abbey, (Bosche Vine-
 yard) Napa, $8.50.
Louis Martini Private Reserve,
 Napa, $5.50.
Louis Martini Regular Bottling,
 Napa, $4.50.
Mayacamas, Napa, $12.00.
Mt. Veeder, Napa, $10.00.
Ridge, (York Creek) Napa, $12.00.
Robert Mondavi Regular Bottling,
 Napa, $8.00.
Robert Mondavi Private Reserve,
 Napa, $20.00.
Rutherford Hill, Napa, $5.00.
Spring Mountain, Napa, $8.50.
Stag's Leap, Napa, $10.00.
Sterling Private Reserve, Napa,
 $20.00.
Stonegate, Napa, $8.50.

REGION B

Alexander Valley, Sonoma, $5.50.
Buena Vista Cask Reserve,
 Sonoma, $8.00.
Chateau St.Jean, Sonoma, $10.00.
Edmeades, Mendocino, $4.50.
Fetzer (Estate Bottled) Men-
 docino, $6.50.
Foppiano, Sonoma, $5.50.
Kenwood, Sonoma, $8.50.
Parducci, Mendocino, $5.50.
Pedroncelli, Sonoma, $4.00.

Simi, Sonoma, $6.00.
Sonoma Vineyards, (Alexander's Crown) Sonoma, $10.00.
Souverain, North Coast, $4.95.

REGION C

Almaden, Monterey, $4.50.
Charles LeFranc, Monterey, $4.00.
Concannon, Alameda, $9.00.
David Bruce, Santa Cruz, $7.50.
Estrella River, San Luis Obispo, $7.00.
Firestone, Santa Barbara, $6.50.
Fortino, Santa Clara, $5.50.
Hoffman Mountain Ranch, San Luis Obispo, $10.00.
Mirassou Harvest Selection, Monterey, $6.50.
Monterey Peninsula, Monterey, $4.75. ·
Ridge, (Monte Bello) Santa Clara, $10.00.
Sherrill Cellars, (Gilroy) Santa Clara, $6.00.
Zaca Mesa, Santa Barbara, $6.50.

REGION D

Colony, California, $1.89.
Growers, California, $1.49.
Montevina, Amador, $5.00.
Rancho Yerba Buena, Madera, $3.50.
Shenandoah, Amador, $6.50.

# Carignane

REGION B

Fetzer, Mendocino, $2.75.
Parducci, Mendocino, $3.50.
Simi, Sonoma, $2.95.

# Chablis

REGION A

Charles Krug, California, $3.00.
Louis Martini, California, $2.90.

REGION B

Buena Vista, North Coast, $3.75.

REGION C

Paul Masson, California, $2.49.
San Martin, California, $2.10.
Wente, California, $2.75.

REGION D

Guasti, $2.00.
M. LaMont, California, $1.79.

# Chablis Blanc

REGION D

Gallo, California, $1.87.

# Champagne

REGION A

Beaulieu Champagne de Chardonnay, Napa, $9.92.
Domaine Chandon Napa Valley Blanc de Noir, Napa, $10.40.
Domaine Chandon Napa Valley Brut, Napa, $10.40.
Hanns Kornell Sehr Trocken, California, $11.50.
Schramsberg Blanc de Blanc, Napa, $9.50.
Schramsberg Cuvée de Gamay, Napa, $8.85.

REGION B

Chateau St. Jean Blanc de Noir, Sonoma, $9.50.
Korbel Brut, California, $7.00.

REGION C

Almaden Blanc de Blanc, California, $7.25.

## Charbono

REGION A

Inglenook, Napa, $5.50.

REGION B

Souverain, North Coast, $4.00.

REGION C

Fortino, Santa Clara, $4.50.

## Chardonnay

REGION A

Beringer, Napa, $6.50.
Burgess, Napa, $9.75.
Chappellet, Napa, $10.00.
Chateau Montelena, Napa, $10.00.
Christian Brothers, Napa, $4.75.
Cuvaison, Napa, $8.00.
Freemark Abbey, Napa, $9.75.
Heitz, Napa, $15.00.
Joseph Phelps, Napa, $8.75.
Mayacamas, Napa, $9.00.
Mt. Veeder, Napa, $18.00.
Robert Mondavi, Napa, $10.00.
Spring Mountain, Napa, $8.50.
Sterling, Napa, $10.00.
Stonegate, Napa, $8.00.
Stony Hill, Napa, $8.00.

Trefethen, Napa, $7.50.
Villa Mt. Eden, Napa, $10.00.

REGION B

Alexander Valley, Sonoma, $7.50.
Buena Vista, (Estate Bottled) Sonoma, $8.00.
Chateau St. Jean, (Robert Young Vineyard) Sonoma, $10.00.
Davis Bynum, Sonoma, $7.50.
Dehlinger, Sonoma, $7.50.
Dry Creek, Sonoma, $8.00.
Edmeades, Mendocino, $6.50.
Gundlach-Bundschu, Sonoma $10.00.
Hanzell, Sonoma, $10.00.
Husch, Mendocino, $7.50.
Joseph Swan, Sonoma, $10.00.
Korbel, Sonoma, $5.25.
Parducci, Mendocino, $6.00.
River Oaks, Sonoma, $5.49.
Simi, Sonoma, $7.00.
Sonoma Vineyards, (River West) Sonoma, $7.25.
Veedercrest, Sonoma, $9.50.

REGION C

Barengo, Santa Barbara, $5.25.
Chalone, Monterey, $5.75.
David Bruce, Santa Cruz, $4.50.
Estrella River, San Luis Obispo, $7.50.
Firestone, Santa Barbara, $7.50.
Hoffman Mountain Ranch, (Edna Valley) San Luis Obispo, $8.50.
Jekel, Monterey, $7.00.
Mirassou Harvest Selection, Monterey, $6.50.
Z-D, Santa Barbara, $10.00.

REGION D

Angelo Papagni, Madera, $6.00.

REGION E

Franciscan, (Temecula) Riverside, $7.49.

## Chenin Blanc

REGION A

Chappellet, Napa, $6.00.
Charles Krug, Napa, $4.00.
Franciscan, Napa, $3.25.
Robert Mondavi, Napa, $5.25.
Sonoma Vineyards, Sonoma, $3.90.

REGION B

Alexander Valley, Sonoma, $5.00.
Cambiaso, Sonoma, $4.00.
Grand Cru, Yolo, $4.75.
Johnson's Alexander Valley, Sonoma, $3.75.
Kenwood, Sonoma, $4.75.
Landmark, Sonoma, $4.50.
Parducci, Mendocino, $4.00.
Sonoma Vineyards, Sonoma, $3.90.

REGION C

Bargetto, Santa Cruz, $1.99.
Hoffman Mountain Ranch, San Luis Obispo, $4.50.
J. Lohr, Monterey, $3.50.
Novitiate, Santa Clara, $3.25.

REGION D

Angelo Papagni Sparkling Chenin Blanc, Madera, $5.50.

REGION E

Callaway, Riverside, $4.75.
San Pasqual, San Diego, $4.50.

## Chianti

REGION A

Louis Martini, California, $2.90.

## Emerald Riesling

REGION D

Angelo Papagni Late Harvest, Madera, $6.50.

## Folle Blanche

REGION A

Louis Martini, Napa, $4.25.

## French Colombard

REGION A

Gavilan, Napa, $3.99.
Robert Pecota, Napa, $4.00.

REGION B

Mark West, Sonoma, $3.75.
Sonoma Vineyards, Sonoma, $3.11.
Souverain, North Coast, $3.00.

REGION D

Ambassador, California, $1.89.
Gallo, California, $1.99.
Giumarra, California, $1.53.
Guasti, California, $1.99.
Guild, California, $1.99.
M. LaMont, California, $1.89.

## Fumé Blanc

REGION A

Christian Brothers, Napa, $4.60.
Robert Mondavi, Napa, $6.75.

REGION B

Chateau St. Jean, Sonoma, $6.50.
Dry Creek, Sonoma, $6.00.
Souverain, North Coast, $5.00.

# Gamay

REGION A

Robert Mondavi, Napa, $4.50.

REGION B

Mill Creek, Sonoma, $3.75.
Pedroncelli, Sonoma, $3.00.
Trentadue, Sonoma, $2.75.

REGION C

J. Lohr, Monterey, $3.50.

REGION E

San Pasqual, San Diego, $4.00.

# Gamay Beaujolais

REGION A

Charles Krug, Napa, $3.75.
Robert Pecota, Napa, (Nouveau),
   $4.25.
Stag's Leap, Napa, $3.50.

REGION B

Parducci, Mendocino, $3.50.

REGION C

Monterey Vineyard, Monterey,
   $4.00.
Weibel, Alameda, $3.50.

# Gewurztraminer

REGION A

Charles Krug, Napa, $5.00.
Christian Brothers, Napa, $6.00.
Joseph Phelps, Napa, $4.75.
Rutherford Hill, Napa, $4.50.
Villa Mt. Eden, Napa, $5.00.

REGION B

Buena Vista, Sonoma, $5.99.
Chateau St. Jean, Sonoma, $6.75.
Clos du Bois, Sonoma, $5.50.
Edmeades, Mendocino, $5.95.
Geyser Peak, Sonoma, $5.25.
Grand Cru, (Garden Creek Ranch)
   Sonoma, $7.50.
Hacienda, Sonoma, $6.00.
Hop Kiln, Sonoma, $5.50.
Husch, Mendocino, $6.00.
Pedroncelli, Sonoma, $4.37.

REGION C

Almaden, Monterey, $3.75.
Cresta Blanca, San Luis Obispo,
   $3.50.
Firestone, Santa Barbara, $5.00.
Mirassou, Santa Clara, $4.75.
Monterey Vineyard, Monterey,
   $4.75.
Z-D, Santa Barbara, $5.00.

REGION D

Gallo, California, $3.19.
M. LaMont, California, $1.89.

# Green Hungarian

REGION B

Buena Vista, Sonoma, $3.72.
Sebastiani, North Coast, $3.75.

REGION C

Weibel, Alameda, $5.85.

## Grenache Rosé

REGION B

Sonoma Vineyards, Sonoma, $3.90.

REGION C

Almaden, San Benito, $1.80.

## Grey Riesling

REGION C

Wente, Alameda, $4.00.

## Grignolino

REGION A

Beringer, Napa, $3.75.
Heitz, Napa, $5.00.

## Johannisberg Riesling

REGION A

Beaulieu, (Beauclair) Napa, $5.00.
Beringer, Napa, $5.50.
Burgess, (Winery Lake) Napa, $8.50.
Chappellet, Napa, $6.00.
Chateau Montelena, North Coast, $5.50.
Freemark Abbey, Napa, $4.50.
Freemark Abbey Sweet Select, Napa, $9.00.
Heitz, Napa, $5.50.
Joseph Phelps, Napa, $5.00.
Long Vineyard, Botrytised, Napa, $9.00.

Rutherford Hill, Napa, $4.50.
Trefethen, Napa, $6.00.

REGION B

Alexander Valley, Sonoma, $4.25.
Buena Vista, Sonoma, $8.00.
Chateau St. Jean, Selected Late Harvest, (Belle Terre Vineyard) Sonoma, $10.00.
Chateau St. Jean Individual Dry Bunch Selected, (Belle Terre Vineyard) Sonoma, $25.00 (half bottle).
Clos du Bois, Sonoma, $5.50.
Geyser Peak, Sonoma, $5.00.
Hacienda, Sonoma, $9.00.
Landmark, Sonoma, $5.00.
Simi, Sonoma, $6.00.
Sonoma Vineyards, (LeBaron), Sonoma, $9.75.
Souverain, North Coast, $4.49.

## Late-Harvest Riesling

REGION C

Concannon, Alameda, $4.75.
Felton-Empire, (Santa Maria) San Luis Obispo, $8.00.
Firestone, Santa Barbara, $5.00.
Hoffman Mountain Ranch, San Luis Obispo, $5.50.
Jekel, Monterey, $5.00.
Mirassou, Monterey, $4.25.
Monterey Vineyard, Monterey, $2.95.
Zaca Mesa, Santa Barbara, $3.95.

REGION D

Gallo, California, $2.79.

# Le Blanc de Blanc

REGION C

Wente, Monterey, $3.25.

# Merlot

REGION A

Stag's Leap Wine Cellars, Napa, $9.00.
Sterling, Napa, $8.00.

REGION B

Gundlach-Bundschu, Sonoma, $6.00.

REGION C

Z-D, San Luis Obispo, $9.00.

# Monterey Riesling

REGION C

Mirassou, Monterey, $3.95.

# Muscat Blanc

REGION A

Inglenook, Napa Valley, $4.00.

REGION C

Concannon, Alameda, $4.50.

# Muscat Canelli

REGION C

Estrella River, San Luis Obispo, $5.50.

# Petite Rosé

REGION C

Mirassou, Monterey, $3.25.

# Petite Sirah

REGION A

Caneros Creek, Napa, $6.50.
Freemark Abbey, (York Creek) Napa, $6.00.

REGION B

Field Stone, Sonoma, $8.50.
Foppiano, Sonoma, $4.00.
Hop Kiln, Sonoma, $8.00.
Kenwood, Sonoma, $4.50.
Parducci, Mendocino, $4.50.
Sonoma Vineyards, Sonoma, $4.40.
Souverain, North Coast, $4.49.

REGION C

Ahlgren, Monterey, $6.00.
Concannon, California, $4.00.
Mirassou, Monterey, $4.19.
Pedrizzetti, San Luis Obispo, $3.75.
San Martin, Monterey, $4.00.

REGION E

Assumption Abbey, Riverside, $4.00.
Callaway, Riverside, $6.75.

# Pinot Blanc

REGION A

Inglenook, Napa, $4.50.

REGION B

Chateau St. Jean, Sonoma, $5.00.
Fetzer, Mendocino, $6.00.

REGION C

Chalone, Monterey, $5.00.
J. Lohr, Monterey County, $4.50.
Roudon-Smith, Monterey, $6.50.
Wente, Monterey, $4.50.

## Pinot Noir

REGION A

Beaulieu, Napa, $4.50.
Beringer, Napa, $5.00.
Carneros Creek, Napa, $10.00.
Caymus, Napa, $7.00.
Freemark Abbey, Napa, $6.00.
Raymond, Napa, $6.50.
Robert Mondavi, Napa, $6.50.
Rutherford Hill, Napa, $4.50.
Sterling, Napa, $6.00.

REGION B

Buena Vista, Sonoma, $5.00.
Davis Bynum, Sonoma, $5.50.
Grand Cru, Sonoma, $5.00.
Gundlach-Bundschu, Sonoma, $7.00.
Husch, Mendocino, $7.50.
Joseph Swan, Sonoma, $6.50.
J. W. Morris, Sonoma, $6.00.
Parducci, Mendocino, $5.00.
Sonoma Vineyards Estate Bottled, Sonoma, $6.50.
Souverain, North Coast, $4.25.

REGION C

Chalone, Monterey, $5.00.
David Bruce, Santa Cruz, $5.50.

Hoffman Mountain Ranch, San Luis Obispo, $15.00.
J. Lohr, Monterey County, $6.00.
Mirassou, Monterey, $5.00.
Monterey Vineyard, Monterey, $6.00.
Novitiate, Santa Clara, $3.75.
San Martin, Monterey, $4.50.

## Pinot Noir (Nouveau)

REGION A

Rutherford Hill, Napa, $4.00.

## Pinot St. George

REGION A

Christian Brothers, Napa, $6.00.

## Rkatsiteli

REGION C

Concannon, Livermore, $4.50.

## Sauvignon Blanc

REGION A

Joseph Phelps, Napa, $6.50.
Pope Valley, Napa, $4.50.
Sterling, Napa, $6.00.
Stonegate, Napa, $6.50.

REGION B

Chateau St. Jean, (Pat Paulsen Vineyard) Sonoma, $7.50.
Dry Creek, Sonoma, $6.50.
Foppiano Sonoma Fumé, Sonoma, $6.00.
Preston, Sonoma, $6.50.

REGION C

Concannon, Alameda, $5.25.
Estrella River, San Luis Obispo, $4.75.
Monterey Vineyard, Monterey, $10.00.
Santa Ynez Valley, Santa Barbara, $6.00.

REGION D

Gallo, California, $2.39.

REGION E

San Pasqual, San Diego, $4.75.

## Syrah

REGION A

Joseph Phelps, Napa, $6.00.

## Thompson Seedless

REGION C

Thomas Kruse "Chutzpah," $4.00.

## White Burgundy

REGION C

Mirassou, Monterey, $4.99.

## White Riesling

REGION A

Franciscan, Napa, $5.99.
Stony Hill, Napa, $7.50.
Trefethen, Napa, $3.95.

REGION C

Z-D, Santa Barbara, $5.50.

## Zinfandel

REGION A

Chateau Montelena, North Coast, $6.00.
Christian Brothers, Napa, $3.50.
Clos du Val, Napa, $7.50.
Cuvaison, Napa, $4.50.
Louis Martini, California, $4.00.
Raymond, Napa, $5.50.
Sterling, Napa, $6.00.

REGION B

Buena Vista, Sonoma, $4.25.
Burgess, Sonoma, $6.50.
Cuvaison, Napa, $4.50.
Dehlinger, Sonoma, $5.50.
Dry Creek, Sonoma, $5.25.
Fetzer, Mendocino, $5.50.
Foppiano, Sonoma, $4.00.
Grand Cru, Sonoma, $3.95.
Hop Kiln, Sonoma, $4.50.
Johnson's Alexander Valley, Sonoma, $6.50.
Joseph Swan, Sonoma, $7.50.
Kenwood, Sonoma, $5.50.
Lytton Springs, Sonoma, $6.50.
Parducci, Mendocino, $3.50.
Preston, Sonoma, $5.50.
Ridge, (York Creek) Sonoma, $6.50.
Sebastiani, North Coast, $3.75.
Souverain, Sonoma, $3.50.

REGION C

Bargetto, Santa Cruz, $1.79.
Calera Zin, San Luis Obispo, $6.00.
Calera, California, $3.75.
David Bruce, Santa Cruz, $4.50.
Enz, San Benito, $4.00.

Monterey Vineyard December
Harvest, Monterey, $3.95.

Ridge, (Paso Robles) San Luis
Obispo, $5.00.

Roudon-Smith, Santa Cruz, $5.00.

San Martin, Monterey, $3.50.

Thomas Kruse, Santa Clara,
$4.50.

Zaca Mesa, Santa Barbara, $4.50.

REGION D

Franzia, California, $1.69.

M. LaMont, California, $1.89.

Montevina Special Selection,
Amador, $6.00.

Shenandoah, Amador, $4.75.

REGION E

Callaway, Riverside, $5.50.

# Vintners' Pride

The winemaker's special delights are not always a well-kept secret to be ferreted out by a wealthy and devoted connoisseur. Many wineries follow the practice of creating a special "Reserve" or "Cellarmaster's Choice" label for exceptional wines. Others provide special information on the back label, saluting a certain vintage or particular growing area or vineyard.

The choices for the following section were particularly hard to make, since the winemaker or winery officer was asked to recommend favorites that are currently available. Among the white wines, which move into and out of the market very rapidly these days, a list can go out of date in a matter of months. And for a small winery whose production may amount to a limited number of cases, a noted wine can take off and be sold out in a few days.

The following list, organized by region, was put together with love by the individuals who create the wines. It is presented without further comment, as there can be none since here you have the experts.

# Napa County
## Region A

ALATERA VINEYARDS
Bruce Newlan, President: 1977 Paradis de Napa Valley Pinot Noir (White Pinot Noir) and 1977 Pinot Noir.

ALTA VINEYARD CELLAR
Ben Falk, owner: 1978 Chardonnay.

BEAULIEU VINEYARDS
Tom Selfridge, winemaker: Cabernet Sauvignon and 1977 Pinot Chardonnay.

BECKETT CELLARS
John Beckett, owner: 1975 Cabernet Sauvignon and 1978 Johannisberg Riesling.

BERINGER VINEYARDS
Myron S. Nightingale, Sr., winemaker: 1977 Chardonnay and 1978 Johannisberg Riesling.

BURGESS CELLARS
Thomas Burgess, owner/winemaker: 1976 Cabernet Sauvignon Vintage Selection and 1977 Pinot Noir.

CAKEBREAD CELLARS
Bruce Cakebread, owner/-winemaker: Sauvignon Blanc and Chardonnay.

CASSAYRE-FORNI CELLARS
Michael J. Forni, part-owner/ winemaker: 1977 Cabernet Sauvignon and 1979 Chenin Blanc.

CAYMUS VINEYARDS
Charles Wagner, president and Randall Dunn, winemaker: 1976 Cabernet Sauvignon and 1976 Pinot Noir.

CHAPPELLET VINEYARD
Tony Soter, winemaker: 1976 Cabernet Sauvignon and 1978 Chenin Blanc.

CHARLES F. SHAW VINEYARD
Charles F. Shaw, Jr., owner/ winemaker: Napa Valley Gamay.

CHARLES KRUG WINERY
Peter Mondavi, president/ winemaker: 1973 Vintage Select Cabernet and Chardonnay.

CHATEAU CHEVALIER WINERY
Greg Bissonette, owner/winemaker: 1975 Cabernet Sauvignon and 1977 Pinot Noir.

CLOS DU VAL WINE COMPANY, LTD. Bernard Portet, winemaker: 1975 Cabernet Sauvignon and 1975 Zinfandel.

CONN CREEK WINERY
John Henderson, winemaker: Cabernet Sauvignon and Chardonnay.

CUVAISON WINERY
Philip Togni, winemaker: 1977 Chardonnay and 1975 Cabernet Sauvignon.

DIAMOND CREEK VINEYARDS
Al Brounstein, owner/winemaker: 1977 Cabernet Sauvignon.

DUCKHORN WINERY
Thomas Rinaldi, winemaker: Napa Valley Merlot.

FLORA SRINGS WINE CO.
Stephen A. Cisler III, winemaker: Chardonnay.

FRANCISCAN VINEYARDS
Justin Meyer, winemaker: 1974 Napa Valley Charbono and 1975 Napa Valley Cabernet Sauvignon.

FREEMARK ABBEY WINERY
Larry Langbehn, winemaker: 1977 Chardonnay and 1975 Cabernet Bosche (Cabernet Sauvignon).

GRGICH HILLS CELLAR
Mike Grgich, president/winemaker: 1977 Chardonnay and 1978 Johannisberg Riesling.

HEITZ WINE CELLARS
Joe Heitz, owner/winemaker: 1974 Pinot Chardonnay and 1975 Cabernet Sauvignon (Fay Vineyards).

INGLENOOK VINEYARDS
Tom Ferrell, winemaker: 1973 Charbono and Blanc de Noir.

JOSEPH PHELPS VINEYARDS
Walter Schug, winemaker: 1975 Cabernet Sauvignon (Eisele Vineyard) and 1977 Johannisberg Riesling (Selected Late Harvest).

LOUIS M. MARTINI WINERY
Michael R. Martini, winemaker: 1976 Cabernet Sauvignon, and 1976 Merlot.

MAYACAMAS VINEYARDS
Bob Travers, owner/winemaker: 1975 Cabernet Sauvignon and 1976 Chardonnay.

MONT LA SALLE VINEYARDS
Brother Timonty, winemaker: 1975 Pinot St. George and 1975 Cabernet Sauvignon.

MT. VEEDER WINERY
Michael A. Bernstein, winemaker: Cabernet Sauvignon and Chenin Blanc.

NAPA VINTNERS
Donald C. Ross, president/winemaker: 1978 Sauvignon Blanc and 1975 Cabernet Sauvignon.

NAPA WINE CELLARS
Charles Woods, owner/winemaker: Chardonnay and Zinfandel.

POPE VALLEY WINERY
Steve Devitt, winemaker: 1977 Napa Valley Cabernet Sauvignon (Spring Lane Vineyards) and 1978 Chenin Blanc.

RIVER BEND WINERY
Tom Cottrell, winemaker: Cabernet Sauvignon and Johannisberg Riesling.

ROBERT KEENAN WINERY
Joseph Cafaro, winemaker: 1977 Cabernet Sauvignon and 1978 Chardonnay.

ROBERT MONDAVI WINERY
Mike Mondavi, president: 1974 Cabernet Sauvignon Reserve and 1978 Fumé Blanc.

ROBERT PECOTA WINERY
Robert Pecota, owner/winemaker: 1979 Gamay Beaujolais and 1979 Sauvignon Blanc.

ROUND HILL CELLARS
Doug Manning, winemaker: 1978 Napa Valley Chardonnay and 1979 Gewurztraminer.

RUTHERFORD HILL WINERY
Phillip Baxter, winemaker: 1978 Gewurztraminer and 1976 Pinot Noir.

V. SATTUI WINERY
Daryl Sattui, owner/winemaker: 1976 Cabernet Sauvignon and 1978 Riesling.

ST. CLEMENT VINEYARDS
Chuck Ortman, winemaker: 1978 Chardonnay and 1977 Cabernet Sauvignon.

SCHRAMSBERG VINEYARDS
Harold Osborne, winemaker: 1974 Blanc de Noirs.

SILVER OAK CELLARS
Justin Meyer, winemaker: 1975 Cabernet Sauvignon.

SMITH-MADRONE VINEYARDS
Stuart and Charles Smith, winemakers: 1977 Johannisberg Riesling.

SPRING MOUNTAIN VINEYARDS
Michael Robbins, owner: Cabernet Sauvignon and Chardonnay.

STAG'S LEAP WINE CELLARS
Warren Winiarski, partner/winemaker: 1976 Cabernet

Sauvignon and 1977 Chardonnay (Haynes Vineyard).

STAG'S LEAP WINERY
Carl Doumani, president: 1974 Petite Syrah and 1976 Burgundy.

STERLING VINEYARDS
Theo Rosenbrand, winemaker, Sergio Traverso-Rueda, oenologist: 1975 Sterling Reserve Cabernet Sauvignon and 1978 Sauvignon Blanc.

STONEGATE WINERY
James and Barbara Spaulding, owners: 1976 Napa Valley Cabernet and 1978 Estate Bottled Sauvignon Blanc.

SUTTER HOME WINERY, INC.
Louis (Bob) Trinchero, president/winemaker: 1976 Amador County Zinfandel and White Zinfandel.

TREFETHEN VINEYARDS
Janet Trefethen, part-owner: 1977 Chardonnay and Eschol Red.

TULOCAY WINERY
W.C. Cadman, partner/winemaker: 1976 Pinot Noir Napa Valley and 1975 Amador County Zinfandel.

VILLA MT. EDEN WINERY
Nils Venge, winemaker: Cabernet Sauvignon and Chardonnay.

VOSE VINEYARDS
Hamilton Vose, president: Chardonnay and Zinblanca.

Z-D WINES
Norman de Leuze, Gino Zepponi, owners/winemakers: 1977 Napa Pinot Noir (Carneros) and 1978 Santa Barbara Chardonnay (Tepusquet Vineyard).

## Solano County
Region A

DIABLO VISTA WINERY
Leon Borowski, winemaker: 1977 Sonoma Zinfandel.

## Humboldt County
Region B

WILLOW CREEK VINEYARDS
Dean Williams, owner/winemaker: 1978 Petite Sirah.

WITTWER WINERY
Roy Wittwer, owner/winemaker: Cabernet Sauvignon.

## Lake County
Region B

KONOCTI CELLARS
William Pease, winemaker: Cabernet Sauvignon Blanc and Zinfandel.

## Marin County
Region B

FAR NIENTE WINERY
Gil Nickel, winemaker: 1979 Napa Valley Chardonnay.

PACHECO RANCH WINERY
Jamie Meves, winemaker: Cabernet Sauvignon.

WOODBURY WINERY
Russell Woodbury, owner/winemaker: 1977 Woodbury Vintage Port.

## Mendocino County
Region B

CRESTA BLANCA WINERY
John Taddeucci, vice president: 1978 Gewurztraminer and Zinfandel.

EDMEADES VINEYARDS
Jed Steele, winemaker: 1978 Rain Wine (Anderson Valley) and 1978 Opal (White Pinot Noir).

FETZER VINEYARDS
Paul E. Dolan, III, winemaker: 1978 Chardonnay and 1977 Estate Bottled Cabernet Sauvignon.

HUSCH VINEYARDS
Alfred White, winemaker: 1978 Pinot Chardonnay and Johannisberg Riesling.

MCDOWELL VALLEY VINEYARDS
George F. Bursick, winemaker: Chenin Blanc and Grenache.

MILANO WINERY
James Milone, Gregory Graziano, owners/winemakers: 1977 Cabernet Sauvignon and 1978 Chardonnay.

NAVARRO WINERY
Ted Bennett, owner/winemaker: 1978 Gewurztraminer and 1978 Chardonnay.

PARDUCCI WINE CELLARS
John Parducci, owner/winemaker: Petite Sirah and Chenin Blanc.

TYLAND VINEYARDS
Dick G. Tijsseling, owner/winemaker: Mendocino Pinot Chardonnay and Mendocino Gamay Beaujolais.

## Sonoma County
## Region B

ALEXANDER VALLEY VINEYARDS
Hank Wetzel, winemaker: Johannisberg Riesling and Chardonnay.

BUENA VISTA WINERY
Richard Williams, winemaker: 1975 Pinot Noir (Cask 8) and 1978 Gewurztraminer.

CAMBIASO WINERY
Robert Fredson, winemaker: Chenin Blanc and Petite Sirah.

CHATEAU ST. JEAN
Richard Arrowood, winemaker: 1978 Sonoma County Chardonnay (Robert Young Vineyard) and 1978 Johannisberg Riesling (*Trockenbeerenauslese*).

DAVIS BYNUM WINERY
Gary Farrell, winemaker: 1978 Allen/Haffner Chardonnay and 1977 Pinot Noir.

DRY CREEK VINEYARD
David Stare, owner/winemaker: 1979 Chenin Blanc and 1977 Cabernet Sauvignon.

FIELD STONE WINERY
Deborah Cutter, winemaker: 1979 Spring Cabernet and 1979 Chenin Blanc.

FOPPIANO WINE COMPANY
Rod Foppiano, winemaker: 1976 Petite Sirah and 1978 Sonoma Fumé.

GEYSER PEAK WINERY
Armand Bussone, winemaker: Estate Bottled 1978 Sonoma County Fumé Blanc and 1976 Sonoma County Pinot Noir.

GRAND CRU VINEYARDS
Robert L. Magnani, winemaker: 1978 Late-Picked Gewurztraminer and 1976 Late-Picked Zinfandel.

GUNDLACH-BUNDSCHU WINERY
John Merritt, Jr., winemaker: Gewurztraminer and Zinfandel.

HACIENDA WINE CELLARS
Steve MacRostie, winemaker: 1978 Gewurztraminer and 1978 Chardonnay.

HOP KILN WINERY
Dr. Martin Griffin, owner/winemaker: 1978 Gewurztraminer and 1977 Petite Sirah.

HORIZON WINERY
Paul Gardner, winemaker: 1977 Zinfandel.

IRON HORSE VINEYARDS
Forrest Tancer, winemaker: 1978 Chardonnay Estate Grown.

ITALIAN SWISS COLONY
Tom Eddy, winemaker: 1978 Cabernet Sauvignon and Crystal Chablis.

J. J. HARASZTHY & SON
Jan Haraszthy, owner: 1975 Zinfandel and 1978 Gewurztraminer.

JOHNSON'S ALEXANDER VALLEY WINERY
Tom Johnson, winemaker: 1978 Late Harvest Zinfandel and 1976 Cabernet Sauvignon.

KENWOOD VINEYARDS
John Sheela, part-owner/business manager: 1976 Zinfandel and 1977 Chardonnay.

KORBEL CHAMPAGNE CELLARS
Jim Huntsinger, winemaker: Blanc de Noir.

LA CREMA VINERA
Rod Berglund, winemaker: 1979 Winery Lake Chardonnay and 1979 Winery Lake Pinot Noir.

LANDMARK VINEYARDS
Bill Mabry, partner/winemaker: 1978 Chardonnay and 1978 Chenin Blanc.

LYTTON SPRINGS WINERY
Walt Walters, president/winemaker: 1978 Zinfandel.

MARK WEST VINEYARDS
Joan Ellis, co-owner/winemaker: Gewurztraminer and Chardonnay.

MARTINI AND PRATI WINES
Frank J. Vannucci, winemaker: Zinfandel and Cabernet Sauvignon.

MATANZAS CREEK WINERY
Merry Edwards, winemaker: 1978 Sonoma Valley Gewurztraminer and 1978 Santa Cruz Mountains Pinot Blanc.

MILL CREEK VINEYARDS
Bob Kreck, winemaker: Cabernet Sauvignon Blush and Merlot.

NERVO WINERY
Armand Bussone, winemaker: Winterchill White and Farmer's Red Table Wine.

J. PEDRONCELLI WINERY
John Pedroncelli, winemaker: 1976 Cabernet Sauvignon and 1978 Gewurztraminer.

A. RAFANELLI WINERY
Americo Rafanelli, winemaker: Zinfandel and Gamay Beaujolais.

ROBERT STEMMLER WINERY
Robert Stemmler, owner/winemaker: Chardonnay and Cabernet Sauvignon.

RUSSIAN RIVER VINEYARDS
Michael Topolos, winemaker: Chardonnay and Cabernet Sauvignon.

SAUSAL WINERY
Dave Demostene, winemaker: 1975 Zinfandel and Sausal Blanc.

SEBASTIANI VINEYARDS
Sam Sebastiani, president/ winemaker: Pinot Noir Blanc and 1977 Chardonnay.

SIMI WINERY
Zelma Long, winemaker: 1973 Cabernet Sauvignon (Private Reserve) and Zinfandel.

SONOMA VINEYARDS
Rodney D. Strong, winemaker: 1976 Alexander's Crown Cabernet Sauvignon and 1978 River West Chardonnay.

SOUVERAIN WINERY
Bill Bonetti, winemaker: Gewurztraminer and Petite Sirah.

TRENTADUE WINERY
Leo Trentadue, winemaker: 1975 Carignane and 1976 Zinfandel.

VALLEY OF THE MOON WINERY
Harry Parducci, winemaker: 1975 Sonoma Valley Pinot Noir and 1978 Estate Bottled Semillon.

WILLOWSIDE VINEYARDS
Berle Beliz, winemaker: 1978 Gewurztraminer and 1978 Pinot Chardonnay.

## Alameda County
Region C

CONCANNON VINEYARD
James Concannon, president: 1975 Petite Sirah and 1978 Johannisberg Riesling; Robert L. Broman, winemaker: Moselle.

MONTCLAIR WINERY
Rick Dove, winemaker: 1976 Cabernet Sauvignon and 1977 Teldeschi Zinfandel.

J. W. MORRIS PORT WORKS
James L. Olsen, winemaker: Founder's Port and Sierra Sabrosa Angelica.

NUMANO SAKE COMPANY
Seizaburo Kawano, sakemaster: Numano Sake and Koshu White Rice Wine.

OAK BARREL WINERY
John Bank, winemaker: Private Stock Port and Chardonnay.

RICHARD CAREY WINERY
Richard Carey, president: Cabernet Sauvignon Special Reserve and Fumé Blanc.

STONY RIDGE WINERY
Harry Rosingane, president: 1977 Ruetz Ranch Zinfandel and 1977 Chardonnay.

VEEDERCREST VINEYARD
A. W. Baxter, winemaker: 1977 Cabernet Sauvignon (Steltzner Vineyard, Napa) and 1978 Chardonnay (Winery Lake Vineyard, Napa); Bob Porter, assistant winemaker: 1978 White Riesling (Late Harvest, Steltzner Vineyard, Napa).

WEIBEL CHAMPAGNE VINEYARDS
Oscar Habluetzel, winemaker and Richard Casqueiro, assistant winemaker: Pinot Chardonnay and Estate Bottled Pinot Noir.

WENTE BROS. WINERY
Eric Wente, president: 1978 Dry Semillon and 1975 Petite Sirah.

## Monterey County
## Region C

JEKEL VINEYARD
Daniel Lee, winemaker: 1978 Chardonnay and 1978 Johannisberg Riesling.

MONTEREY PENINSULA WINERY
Todd Cameron, manager: 1977 Willow Creek Zinfandel (Late Harvest) and 1978 Arroyo Seco Chardonnay.

MONTEREY VINEYARD
Dr. Richard Peterson, winemaker: 1979 Johannisberg Riesling and 1978 Chardonnay.

PAUL MASSON PINNACLES VINEYARD
Joseph Stillman, winemaker: Emerald Dry and Cabernet Sauvignon.

VENTANA VINEYARDS WINERY
Phil Franscioni, winemaker: Chardonnay and Chenin Blanc.

## San Benito County
Region C

CALERA WINE COMPANY
Josh Jensen, president/winemaker: 1977 Zinfandel Templeton and 1976 Zinfandel.

## San Luis Obispo County
## Region C

ESTRELLA RIVER WINERY
W. Gary Eberle, winemaker: 1977 Cabernet Sauvignon and 1978 Chardonnay.

HOFFMAN MOUNTAIN RANCH VINEYARDS
Michael Hoffman, winemaker: 1977 Zinfandel and 1978 Johannisberg Riesling.

LAS TABLAS WINERY
John and Della Mertens, owners: Zinfandel.

LAWRENCE WINERY
James S. Lawrence, winemaker: Chardonnay and Sauvignon Blanc.

MASTANTUONO WINERY
Pasquale Mastan, partner/winemaker: 1977 Zinfandel and 1977 Zinfandel Nuovo.

PESENTI WINERY
Frank Nerelli, Steve Pesenti, winemakers: Zinfandel Blanc and White Burgundy.

YORK MOUNTAIN WINERY
Steve Goldman, winemaker: Merlot.

## San Mateo County
Region C

OBESTER WINERY
Paul Obester, proprietor/winemaker: 1977 Cabernet Sauvignon and 1978 Sauvignon Blanc.

# Santa Barbara County
## Region C

BALLARD CANYON WINERY
Gene Hallock, winemaker:
Cabernet Sauvignon Blanc and
Johannisberg Riesling.

J. CAREY CELLARS
Richard R. Longoria, winemaker: Cabernet Sauvignon
and Cabernet Sauvignon Blanc.

FIRESTONE VINEYARD
Tony Austin, winemaker: 1977
Chardonnay and 1978 Riesling.

RANCHO SISQUOC WINERY
Harold Pfeiffer, winemaker:
1977 Cabernet Sauvignon and
1978 Johannisberg Riesling.

SANTA YNEZ VALLEY WINERY
Fred Brander, winemaker: 1978
Sauvignon Blanc and Chardon-
nay Reserve de Cave.

ZACA MESA WINERY
Ken Brown, winemaker: 1977
Cabernet Sauvignon and 1978
Chardonnay.

# Santa Clara County
## Region C

CASA DE FRUTA
Henry G., Joseph A. and
Eugene A. Zanger, partners:
Gewurztraminer and Zinfandel
Rosé.

CONGRESS SPRINGS VINEYARDS
Daniel Gehrs, winemaker:
Pinot Blanc and Fumé Blanc.

EMILIO GUGLIELMO WINERY
Gene Guglielmo, business
manager: Santa Clara Valley
Claret (Limited Bottling) and
1974 Cabernet Sauvignon.

GEMELLO WINERY, INC.
Mario Gemello, winemaker:
1975 Cabernet Sauvignon and
1974 Zinfandel.

HECKER PASS WINERY
Mario Fortino, winemaker: Petite Sirah and Zinfandel.

LIVE OAKS WINERY
Peter Scagliotti, owner: 1974
Premium Burgundy and Che-
nin Blanc (Medium).

LLORDS AND ELWOOD WINERY
Richard H. Elwood, winemaker:
Velvet Hill Pinot Noir Cuvée 11
and Ancient Proverb Port.

MARTIN RAY WINERY
Peter Martin Ray, presi-
dent/winemaker: Champagne
Cuvée 1977 and La Montana
Pinot Noir Cuvée 3.

MIRASSOU VINEYARDS
Don Alexander, winemaker:
1977 Monterey Zinfandel and
1978 Monterey Chardonnay.

MOUNT EDEN VINEYARDS
Richard L. White, winemaker:
1976 Estate Bottled Cabernet
Sauvignon and 1977 Estate
Bottled Chardonnay.

NOVITIATE WINES
Brother Lee H. Williams, SJ,
winemaker: Johannisberg
Riesling and Black Muscat.

PAUL MASSON VINEYARDS
Elliott Fine, president: Cabernet Sauvignon and Rare Souzao Port.

PEDRIZZETTI WINERY
Ed Pedrizzetti, owner/winemaker: Petite Sirah and Gewurztraminer.

RAPAZZINI WINERY
Jon P. Rapazzini, president: 1977 Gewurztraminer.

RICHERT & SONS WINERY
Scott Richert, winemaker: Richert & Sons Triple Cream Sherry and Richert Cellars Alexander Valley Cabernet Sauvignon.

RONALD LAMB WINERY
Ronald Lamb, owner/winemaker: 1978 Monterey County Napa Gamay and 1978 Dry Johannisberg Riesling.

SAN MARTIN WINERY
Ed Friedrich, winemaker: Chenin Blanc and Chardonnay.

SARAH'S VINEYARD
Marilyn Otteman, partner: Grenache and Zinfandel.

SHERRILL CELLARS
Nat Sherrill, partner/winemaker: 1977 Cabernet Sauvignon and 1976 Chardonnay.

SYCAMORE CREEK VINEYARDS
Terry Parks, partner/winemaker: 1978 Estate Bottled Zinfandel and 1978 Estate Bottled Carignane.

TURGEON & LOHR WINERY
Peter M. Stern, winemaker: Johannisberg Riesling and Monterey Gamay.

## Santa Cruz County Region C

BARGETTO'S SANTA CRUZ WINERY
Lawrence Bargetto, president/winemaker: 1978 Chardonnay and 1976 Cabernet Sauvignon.

DAVID BRUCE WINERY
Steve Millier, winemaker: 1977 Estate Chardonnay and 1977 Edna Valley Chardonnay.

DEVLIN WINE CELLARS
Charles Devlin, owner/winemaker: Pinot Blanc and Zinfandel.

FELTON-EMPIRE VINEYARDS
Leo McCloskey, winemaker: White Riesling and Gewurztraminer.

FRICK WINERY
William R. and Judith Frick, winemakers: 1977 Pinot Noir and 1978 Chardonnay.

RIVER RUN VINTNERS
William and T. J. Hangen, partners/winemakers: 1978 Zinfandel (Morgan Hill) and 1978 Pinot Noir (Ventana Ranch).

ROUDON-SMITH VINEYARDS
Robert Roudon, winemaker: 1976 Chardonnay and 1976 Zinfandel (Chauvet Vineyard).

P AND M STAIGER WINERY
Paul Staiger, winemaker: 1977 Zinfandel and 1976 Cabernet Sauvignon.

## Amador County
Region D

ARGONAUT WINERY
W. M. Bilbo, partner: 1976 Zinfandel and 1977 Barbera.

D'AGOSTINI WINERY
Tulio D'Agostini, partner: 1974 Estate Bottled Zinfandel and Dry Muscat.

KENWORTHY VINEYARDS
John Kenworthy, owner/winemaker: Zinfandel and Cabernet Sauvignon.

MONTEVINA WINES
Cary Gott, owner: 1978 Sauvignon Blanc and 1977 Special Selection Zinfandel.

SANTINO WINERY
Scott Harvey, winemaker: White Zinfandel and White Harvest (semi-dry) Zinfandel.

SHENANDOAH VINEYARDS
Leon E. Sobon, owner/winemaker: Amador County Zinfandel and Amador Cabernet Sauvignon.

STONERIDGE
Gary Porteous, owner/winemaker: 1975 Zinfandel Late Harvest and 1976 Zinfandel Late Harvest.

## Calaveras County
Region D

CHISPA CELLARS
Robert Bliss, partner/winemaker: 1976 Zinfandel and Ruby Cabernet.

STEVENOT VINEYARDS
Barden Stevenot, owner: Chenin Blanc Estate Bottled and 1978 Zinfandel.

## El Dorado County
Region D

BOEGER WINERY
Greg Boeger, owner/winemaker: Cabernet Sauvignon and Zinfandel.

## Fresno County
Region D

B. CRIBARI & SONS WINERY
Albert Cribari, vice president/winemaker: Mendocino Burgundy and Cabernet Sauvignon.

MONT LA SALLE VINEYARD (MT. TIVY WINERY)
Ron Hanson, production manager: Meloso Cream Sherry and Tinta Cream Port.

VILLA BIANCHI WINERY
Nick Chargin, winemaker: Cosa Nostra and Chablis d'Casa.

## Kern County
Region D

GIUMARRA VINEYARDS
Bill Nakata, winemaker: Chenin Blanc and Carnelian.

LAMONT WINERY, INC.
Sam Balakian, winemaker: Gewurztraminer and Pinot Chardonnay.

A. PERELLI-MINETTI & SONS WINERY
George Kolarovich, vice president of production/winemaker: 1978 Chablis and 1977 Zinfandel.

## Madera County
Region D

ANGELO PAPAGNI VINEYARDS
Rosemary Papagni, administrative assistant: 1975 Alicante Bouschet and 1978 Fumé Blanc.

QUADY WINERY
Andrew Quady, owner: 1977 Rancho Tierra Rejada Paso Robles Vintage Port and 1977 Amador County Vintage Port.

## San Joaquin County
Region D

DELICATO VINEYARDS
Hector Castro, winemaker: Green Hungarian and French Colombard.

EAST-SIDE WINERY
Lee Eichele, winemaker: Chenin Blanc and Tinta Madeira Port.

FRANZIA BROTHERS WINERY
Arthur Ciocca, president: Mountain Chablis Blanc and Mountain Rhine.

LUCAS HOME WINE
David Lucas, winemaker: Zinfandel.

## Yolo County
Region D

HARBOR WINERY
Charles H. Myers, winemaker: 1977 Chardonnay and 1976 Mission Del Sol.

## Riverside County
Region E

CILURZO & PICONI WINERY
John Piconi and Vincenzo Cilurzo, owners/winemakers: Cabernet Sauvignon and Petite Sirah.

GALLEANO WINERY, INC.
B. D. (Nino) Galleano, Donald D. Galleano, managers/winemakers: 1977 100 Percent Zinfandel.

MOUNT PALOMAR WINERY
Joseph E. Cherpin, winemaker: 1977 Cabernet Sauvignon and Golden Sherry.

## San Bernardino County
Region E

## San Diego County
Region E

THOMAS VINEYARDS
Joseph A. Filippi, owner/winemaker: Burgundy and Raspberry.

SAN PASQUAL VINEYARDS
Kerry G. Damskey, winemaker: Gamay and Sauvignon Blanc.

# Jug Wines

Jug wine should be reasonably priced, good quality wine that you can pour immediately and drink — and enjoy — with nearly any meal, every day. Jug wines are often a consumer's introduction to wine. As such they can serve very well, particularly the California jug wines bottled in recent years.

Wine in a jug no longer necessarily means wine in a fat, squat bottle with a ring handle. Though *jug* originally designated either a gallon container or one that was larger, in the old days (before state health laws demanded otherwise) the "jug" was usually a purchaser's own bottle, carried to the winery, and filled from the barrel. Old-timers can recall prices as low as thirty-five and fifty cents a gallon. Today, the term *jug* covers a general type of blended wine, produced in volume and packaged in fifths, magnums, half-gallons; or in metric measurements, 750 milliliter, 1.5, 3, and 4 liter sizes. Effective January 1, 1979, all wine bottles had to be in metric sizes. Until stocks are depleted, some of the customary, nonmetric bottles will continue to be available. Below are the contents by ounces of the various size bottles.

| Nonmetric | | Metric | |
|---|---|---|---|
| fifth | 25.6 oz. | 750 ml | 25.5 oz. |
| half-gallon | 64.0 oz. | 1.5 liters (magnum) | 50.7 oz. |
| gallon | 128.0 oz. | 3 liters | 101.4 oz. |
| | | 4 liters | 135.2 oz. |

In addition to the glass bottles, many wineries are featuring the bag-in-a-box (a plastic bag in a corrugated container). The original 1-, 3- and 5-gallon packaging has been replaced by 4-liter, 12-liter and 18-liter boxes, and some wineries produce a 10-liter size as well.

A jug wine can be made of almost anything, and many labels carry a simple Red Wine or White Wine designation. Others more frequently identify the wines as Chablis (white), Burgundy (red), and Vin Rosé (rosé). But a good many wineries have created proprietary names for their jug wines, and a few feature selected varietal grape names, as a preponderance of a certain variety becomes more available, and therefore, less costly to the winery.

Generally, though, a California jug wine will be a generic wine; the label will have one of fourteen wine names, which are just that — names that do not denote the variety of grape used, the style of wine presented, or any other strongly definitive characteristic. Borrowed from various European winegrowing districts, these names can be Burgundy, Chablis, Claret, Champagne, Chianti, Hock, Madeira, Malaga, Moselle, Port, Rhine Wine, Sauterne, Sherry, and Tokay. In front of each of these words, by law, must be some type of geographic designation. Proprietary names are a means of tying a certain wine to a certain winery, with hopes of influencing brand loyalty. For example, Gallo Hearty Burgundy, Boeger Winery Hangtown Red, or the Chablis d'Casa of Villa Bianchi.

In varietal jugs, there are such choices as Grenache Rosé of Live Oaks Winery, Zinfandel from Foppiano, or Konocti Cellars cork-finished Cabernet Sauvignon. With overproduction of grapes, the overall quality of the jug wines increase; in the jug wines produced from the premium red-grape plantings of the late sixties and early seventies, you can assume a high percentage of Pinot Noir or Cabernet Sauvignon grapes in the blend.

One thing you can depend on — once you have found a jug wine or several that suit your taste — you can buy that wine and enjoy it repeatedly. Jug wines are meant for mass consumption and consistency of style and flavor is assured by careful control of the blending.

They are also meant to be consumed when bought, not cellared or aged. According to most experts, jug wines put in a cellar will not improve; in fact they are quite likely to deteriorate. They can also deteriorate if not consumed within a relatively short time after opening. If you like to have a jug of wine around so that you can enjoy a glass with dinner each evening over a long period of time, maybe a little to use in cooking too, your best buy would most likely be a bag-in-the-box. The reason for this is that the plastic pouch collapses against the surface of the wine as each glass is withdrawn; therefore, the wine is not exposed to air, and air is the enemy that can spoil the wine. An unfinished jug of wine can be stored in a refrigerator for several days without significant depreciation in quality, but it is best to decant the unfinished wine into smaller containers.

Distinguished winemaker Louis Martini recommends the proper way to decant partially emptied jugs into screw-top fifths. He observes that if you don't take this step to preserve the quality of your wine, you chance losing any savings you may have gained by a jug purchase in the first place.

1.  Always use a plastic funnel when decanting from the jug into the fifth.

2.  Use plastic caps to seal the wine in the bottles.

3.  Wash the bottles out, let them dry for about an hour, and they are ready to use again.

## JUG WINES BY REGION

### Region A
Napa County

| Winery | Red | Rosé | White |
|---|---|---|---|
| Beringer Vineyards (Los Hermanos) | Burgundy Gamay Beaujolais Cabernet Sauvignon | Vin Rosé | Chablis Chenin Blanc Rhine French Colombard |
| Charles Krug Winery (C. K. Mondavi) | Burgundy Barberone Claret | Vin Rosé | Chablis Sauterne |
| Inglenook Vineyards (Navalle) | Burgundy Zinfandel Ruby Cabernet | Vin Rosé Pinot Noir Rosé | Chablis Rhine Chenin Blanc French Colombard Riesling |
| Louis Martini | Mountain Red | Mountain Vin Rosé | Mountain White |

| WINERY | RED | ROSÉ | WHITE |
|---|---|---|---|
| Robert Mondavi | California Red Table Wine | California Rosé Table Wine | California White Table Wine |
| Round Hill Cellars | Burgundy Cabernet Sauvignon | Rosé | Chablis Chenin Blanc |

## Region B
## Lake County

| WINERY | RED | ROSÉ | WHITE |
|---|---|---|---|
| Konocti Cellars | Cabernet Sauvignon | | |

## Mendocino County

| | RED | ROSÉ | WHITE |
|---|---|---|---|
| Cresta Blanca | Mendocino Burgundy Zinfandel | Grenache Rosé | Blanc de Blanc Mendocino Chablis (V) |
| Fetzer Vineyards | Premium Red | | Premium White |
| Navarro Vineyards | | Vin Rouge | Edelzwicker |
| Parducci Wine Cellars | Vintage Burgundy | Vintage Rosé | Vintage Chablis |

## Sonoma County

| | RED | ROSÉ | WHITE |
|---|---|---|---|
| Cambiaso Vineyards (1852 House) | Burgundy | Vin Rosé | Chablis |
| Foppiano Vineyards | Zinfandel Burgundy | Vin Rosé | Chablis |
| Geyser Peak Winery (Summit) | Burgundy Napa Gamay | Vin Rosé | Chablis Rhine White Riesling |
| Italian Swiss Colony (Colony) | Zinfandel | | Chablis Chenin Blanc French Colombard |
| Johnson's Alexander Valley | J.D. Martin Red | | |

| Winery | Red | Rosé | Whites |
|---|---|---|---|
| Martini & Prati Wines | Burgundy Zinfandel | | Sauterne |
| Nervo Winery | Farmers Red Chianti Burgundy | Vin Rosé | Winterchill Chablis |
| J. Pedroncelli Winery | Sonoma Red | | Sonoma White |
| Souverain Winery | Burgundy | Pinot Noir Rosé | Chablis |
| Valley of the Moon Winery | Burgundy Zinfandel Claret | Vin Rosé | Chablis Semillon |

# Region C
## Alameda County

| Winery | Red | Rosé | White |
|---|---|---|---|
| Oak Barrel Winery | Vin de Montagne | | Chablis Moselle |
| Richard Carey Winery | Zinfandel Cabernet Sauvignon | | Chenin Blanc French Colombard |

## Monterey County

| | | | |
|---|---|---|---|
| Monterey Peninsula Winery | Big Sur Red | | Big Sur White |
| Taylor California Cellars | Burgundy | Rosé | Chablis Rhine |

## San Luis Obispo County

| | | | |
|---|---|---|---|
| Lawrence Winery | Red Table Wine | Rosé Table Wine | White Table Wine |
| Pesenti Winery (FP) | Burgundy Zinfandel | Rosé | Chablis |

## Santa Clara County

| WINERY | RED | ROSÉ | WHITE |
|---|---|---|---|
| Almaden Vineyards | San Benito Zinfandel Monterey Zinfandel Mountain Red Claret Mountain Red Burgundy Mountain Red Chianti Le Domaine Burgundy Le Domaine Centurion | San Benito Grenache Rosé | Chenin Blanc French Colombard Mountain White Chablis Mountain White Sauterne Mountain Rhine Le Domaine Crown Chablis Le Domaine Rhine |
| Gemello Winery | Burgundy Zinfandel | Rosé | Chablis Rhine |
| Live Oaks Winery | Premium Burgundy | Grenache Rosé | Sauterne |
| Paul Masson Winery | Burgundy Barbera Ruby Cabernet | Rosé Gamay Rosé Vin Rosé Sec | Chablis Rhine Dry Sauterne Emerald Dry Rhine Castle |
| Pedrizzetti Winery | Burgundy | Vin Rosé | Chablis |
| San Martin Winery | California Burgundy | California Vin Rosé | California Chablis |

## Santa Cruz County

| | | | |
|---|---|---|---|
| Bargetto's Winery (Santa Cruz Cellars) | Burgundy | Vin Rosé | Chablis Rhine |
| River Run Vintners | Red Wine | | |

## Region D
Calaveras County

| WINERY | RED | ROSÉ | WHITE |
|--------|-----|------|-------|
| Stevenot Vineyards | Red Table Wine | | White Table Wine |

### El Dorado County

| | | | |
|--------|-----|------|-------|
| Boeger Winery | Hangtown Red | | Hangtown White |

### Fresno County

| | | | |
|--------|-----|------|-------|
| B. Cribari & Sons Winery | Vino Rosso<br>Burgundy<br>Mello Burgundy<br>Zinfandel<br>Cabernet<br>  Sauvignon<br>Mendocino<br>  Burgundy | Pink Chablis<br>Vin Rosé<br>Vino Fiammo | Mountain Chablis<br>Rhine<br>French<br>  Colombard<br>Chardonnay<br>Extra Dry Chablis<br>Vino Bianco |
| Villa Bianchi Winery | Burgundy d'Casa | Vin Rosé d'Casa | Chablis d'Casa |

### Kern County

| | | | |
|--------|-----|------|-------|
| Giumarra Vineyards | Burgundy | Vin Rosé | Mountain Chablis<br>Rhine |
| Lamont Winery, Inc. (M. Lamont) | Burgundy | Vin Rosé | Chablis |

### Sacramento County

Gibson Wine Co.     Various fruit and berry wines in jug sizes

### San Joaquin County

Barengo
  Vineyards

DESSERT WINES

| | | | |
|--------|-----|------|-------|
| Dry Sherry<br>Cream Sherry | Zinfandel<br>Petite Sirah | Pink Chablis<br>Gamay Rosé | Dry Semillon<br>French<br>  Colombard |

| WINERY | RED | ROSÉ | WHITE |
|---|---|---|---|
| Tawny Port<br>Crematri<br>Cream of<br>  Marsala<br>Cremocha<br>Ambermint<br>1962 Knoushe<br>Tinta Madeira | Cabernet<br>  Semillon | | Chenin Blanc<br>Muscat<br>  Pantelleria<br>Johannisberg<br>  Riesling<br>Chardonnay |
| Delicato<br>  Vineyards | Burgundy<br>Barberone<br>Zinfandel | Vin Rosé | Chablis Blanc<br>Rhine |

East-Side Winery
(Conti Royale)

DESSERT WINES

Port
Sherry
Pale Dry Sherry
Muscatel
Tokay
White Port
Cream Sherry
Angelica
Tawny Port

| WINERY | RED | ROSÉ | WHITE |
|---|---|---|---|
| (Royal Host) | Burgundy<br>Zinfandel | Vin Rosé<br>Pink Chablis | Haut Sauterne<br>Dry Sauterne<br>Chablis<br>Rhine |
| Franzia Winery | Mountain<br>  Burgundy<br>Franzia Cabernet<br>  Sauvignon | Mountain<br>Grenache Rosé | Mountain Rhine<br>Mountain<br>  Chenin Blanc<br>Franzia French<br>  Colombard<br>Franzia<br>  Chenin Blanc |

## Stanislaus County

| WINERY | RED | ROSÉ | WHITE |
|---|---|---|---|
| E. & J. Gallo<br>  Winery | Hearty<br>  Burgundy<br>Burgundy<br>Chianti | Pink Chablis<br>Vin Rosé | Chablis Blanc<br>Rhine |

## Region E
### Riverside County

| WINERY | RED | ROSÉ | WHITE |
|---|---|---|---|
| Galleano Winery | Burgundy Chianti Vino Rosso Zinfandel | Vin Rosé | Sauterne Chablis Rhine |

DESSERT WINES

Port
Sherry
White Port
Muscatel
Vermouth
Marsala

| | | | |
|---|---|---|---|
| Mount Palomar Winery (Rancho Temecula) | Burgundy | Vin Rosé | Chablis |

### San Bernardino County

| | | | |
|---|---|---|---|
| Thomas Vineyards | Zinfandel Burgundy | Vin Rosé | Sauterne |

DESSERT WINES

Sherry

### San Diego County

| | | | |
|---|---|---|---|
| San Pasqual Vineyards | Red Table Wine | | White Table Wine |

# JUG WINES BY COLOR

## Red — Generic

Almaden Le Domaine Burgundy
Almaden Mountain Red Burgundy
Almaden Mountain Red Chianti
Almaden Mountain Red Claret
Bargetto's Santa Cruz Cellars
  Burgundy
B. Cribari & Sons Burgundy
B. Cribari & Sons Mello Burgundy
B. Cribari & Sons Mendocino
  Burgundy
B. Cribari & Sons Vino Rosso
Beringer Vineyards Los Hermanos
  Burgundy
Boeger Winery Hangtown Red
Cambiaso Vineyards 1852 House
  Burgundy
C. K. Mondavi Burgundy
C. K. Mondavi Claret
Cresta Blanca Mendocino Burgundy
Delicato Burgundy
East-Side Royal Host Burgundy
Fetzer Premium Red
Foppiano Vineyards Burgundy
Franzia Mountain Burgundy
Galleano Winery Burgundy
Galleano Winery Chianti
Galleano Winery Vino Rosso
E. & J. Gallo Burgundy
E. & J. Gallo Chianti
E. & J. Gallo Hearty Burgundy
Gemello Winery Burgundy
Geyser Peak Summit Burgundy
Giumarra Burgundy
Inglenook Navalle Burgundy
Johnson's J. D. Martin Red
LaMont Burgundy
Lawrence Red Table Wine
Live Oaks Premium Burgundy
Louis M. Martini Mountain Red

Martini & Prati Burgundy
Monterey Peninsula Winery
  Big Sur Red
Mount Palomar Winery Rancho
  Temecula Burgundy
Nervo Burgundy
Nervo Chianti
Nervo Farmers Red
Oak Barrel Vin de Montagne
Parducci Vintage Burgundy
Paul Masson Burgundy
Pedrizzetti Burgundy
Pedroncelli Sonoma Red
Pesenti FP Burgundy
River Run Vintners Red Wine
Robert Mondavi California
  Red Table Wine
Round Hill Cellars Burgundy
San Martin California Burgundy
San Pasqual Red Table Wine
Souverain Burgundy
Stevenot Red Table Wine
Taylor California Cellars
  Burgundy
Thomas Vineyards Burgundy
Valley of the Moon Burgundy
Valley of the Moon Claret
Villa Bianchi Burgundy d'Casa

## Red — Varietal

### Barbera

Paul Masson

### Barberone

C. K. Mondavi
Delicato

## Cabernet Sauvignon

B. Cribari & Sons
Beringer Los Hermanos
Franzia
Konocti Cellars
Richard Carey
Round Hill

## Cabernet Semillon

Barengo

## Gamay Beaujolais

Beringer Los Hermanos

## Napa Gamay

Geyser Peak Summit

## Petite Sirah

Barengo

## Ruby Cabernet

Inglenook Navalle
Paul Masson

## Zinfandel

Almaden San Benito
Almaden Monterey
Barengo
B. Cribari & Sons
Cresta Blanca
Delicato
East-Side Winery
Foppiano Winery
Galleano
Gemello
Inglenook Navalle
Italian Swiss Colony
Martini & Prati
Pesenti FP
Richard Carey

Thomas Vineyards
Valley of the Moon

## Rosé — Generic

Barengo Pink Chablis
Bargetto Vin Rosé
B. Cribari & Sons Pink Chablis
B. Cribari & Sons Vino Fiammo
B. Cribari & Sons Vin Rosé
Beringer Vin Rosé
Cambiaso 1852 House Vin Rosé
C. K. Mondavi Vin Rosé
Delicato Vin Rosé
E. & J. Gallo Vin Rosé
E. & J. Gallo Pink Chablis
East-Side Royal Host
   Pink Chablis
East-Side Royal Host Vin Rosé
Foppiano Vin Rosé
Galleano Vin Rosé
Gemello Rosé
Geyser Peak Summit Vin Rosé
Giumarra Vin Rosé
Inglenook Navalle Vin Rosé
LaMont Vin Rosé
Lawrence Rosé Table Wine
Louis M. Martini Mountain
   Vin Rosé
Mount Palomar Vin Rosé
Navarro Vin Rouge
Nervo Vin Rosé
Parducci Vintage Rosé
Paul Masson Rosé
Paul Masson Vin Rosé Sec
Pedrizzetti Vin Rosé
Pesenti FP Rosé
Robert Mondavi California
   Rosé Table Wine
San Martin Vin Rosé
Taylor California Cellars Rosé
Valley of the Moon Vin Rosé
Villa Bianchi Vin Rosé d'Casa

## Rosé — Varietals

### Pinot Noir Rosé

Inglenook Navalle
Souverain

### Grenache Rosé

Almaden (San Benito)
Cresta Blanca
Franzia (Mountain)
Live Oaks

### Gamay Rosé

Almaden (San Benito)
Barengo
Paul Masson

## White — Generic

Almaden Le Domaine
 Crown Chablis
Almaden Le Domaine Rhine
Almaden Mountain Rhine
Almaden Mountain White Chablis
Almaden Mountain
 White Sauterne
Bargetto Chablis
Bargetto Rhine
B. Cribari & Sons
 Mountain Chablis
B. Cribari & Sons Rhine
B. Cribari & Sons
 Extra Dry Chablis
B. Cribari & Sons Vino Bianco
Beringer Los Hermanos Chablis
Beringer Los Hermanos Rhine
Boeger Hangtown Gold
Cambiaso 1852 House Chablis
C. K. Mondavi Chablis
C. K. Mondavi Sauterne
Cresta Blanca Blanc de Blanc

Cresta Blanca Chablis
Delicato Chablis Blanc
Delicato Rhine
East-Side Royal Host Chablis
East-Side Royal Host
 Dry Sauterne
East-Side Royal Host
 Haut Sauterne
East-Side Royal Host Rhine
Fetzer Premium White
Foppiano Chablis
Franzia Mountain Rhine
Galleano Chablis
Galleano Rhine
Galleano Sauterne
E. & J. Gallo Chablis Blanc
E. & J. Gallo Rhine
Gemello Chablis
Gemello Rhine
Geyser Peak Summit Chablis
Geyser Peak Summit Rhine
Giumarra Mountain Chablis
Giumarra Rhine
Inglenook Navalle Chablis
Inglenook Navalle Rhine
LaMont Chablis
Lawrence White Table Wine
Live Oaks Sauterne
Louis M. Martini Mountain White
Martini and Prati Sauterne
Monterey Peninsula Winery
 Big Sur White
Mount Palomar Chablis
Navarro Edelzwicker
Nervo Chablis
Nervo Winterchill
Oak Barrel Chablis
Oak Barrel Moselle
Parducci Vintage Chablis
Paul Masson Chablis
Paul Masson Dry Sauterne
Paul Masson Emerald Dry
Paul Masson Rhine

Paul Masson Rhine Castle
Pedrizzetti Chablis
Pedroncelli Sonoma White
Pesenti FP Chablis
Robert Mondavi California
  White Table Wine
Round Hill Chablis
San Martin California Chablis
San Pasqual White Table Wine
Souverain Chablis
Stevenot White Table Wine
Taylor California Cellars Chablis
Taylor California Cellars Rhine
Thomas Vineyards Sauterne
Valley of the Moon Chablis
Villa Bianchi Chablis d'Casa

## White — Varietal

### Chardonnay

Barengo
B. Cribari & Sons

### Chenin Blanc

Almaden
Barengo
Beringer Los Hermanos
Franzia
Inglenook Navalle
Italian Swiss Colony
Richard Carey
Round Hill

### French Colombard

Almaden
Barengo
B. Cribari & Sons
Beringer Los Hermanos
Franzia
Inglenook Navalle
Italian Swiss Colony
Richard Carey

## Riesling (Johannisberg Riesling, White Riesling)

Barengo (Johannisberg Riesling)
Geyser Peak Summit
  (White Riesling)
Inglenook Navalle (Riesling)

### Semillon

Barengo (Dry Semillon)
Valley of the Moon

# Dessert and Aperitif Wines

## Angelica

East-Side

## Madeira

Barengo

## Marsala

Barengo
Galleano

## Muscat Pantelleria

Barengo

## Muscatel

East-Side
Galleano

## Port

Barengo
East-Side
Galleano

## Sherry

Barengo
East-Side

Galleano
Thomas Vineyards

## Tokay
East-Side

Vermouth
Galleano

# California Champagne

There are, at present, about thirty California wineries that produce champagne by various processes. You would, however, get a stern reprimand from the French for applying their jealously guarded appellation "Champagne" to these sparkling wines. The consumer, however, has enjoyed these champagnes of California as a wine of celebration since the mid-1800s, and this trend shows every indication of growing in the number of consumers and the amounts they drink.

According to *Wines and Vines* annual statistical report, those wineries producing champagne range in size from small family operations turning out fewer than five thousand cases a year to the giants providing five hundred thousand cases and more. Almost two-thirds of these wineries produce their champagne by either the classic French *methode champenoise,* identified on the label by the inscription "Naturally fermented in *this* bottle;" or by the transfer method, indicated by the label, "Fermented in *the* bottle." The balance, which includes almost all the high-volume producers, prepare their champagne by the bulk process and label it, usually, "Charmat." In bottle size, California champagnes are available in a 187-ml split, for a "here's to me" celebration; a 375-ml "champagne for two"; the most popular 750 ml for small dinner parties; and the larger magnum, and in a few instances, the double magnum, for large groups and very special occasions.

The recorded history of champagne making in California goes back to the 1850s, when Benjamin D. Wilson, a Los Angeles *vigneron,* is credited with producing the first champagne. He was followed closely by the Sansevain brothers, proprietors of the winery originally owned by Jean Louis Vignes, whom history regards as the first person to make the production of wine a business in California. Meantime, at Buena Vista Winery in Sonoma County, Arpad Haraszthy had been conducting his own experiments with champagne and was racking up a long line of failures. The wine received good reviews and was selling in all the markets it entered, but it was not until 1867 that it could be called a successful wine. In that year it was entered at the Paris Universal Exposition, and the Buena Vista Viticultural Society champagne was awarded an honorable mention.

By the late 1800s California champagne was one of the most important types of wine sold commercially by the state's producers. Eastern cities and foreign export called for great quantities, and experts were beginning to suggest that California's champagne was as good as all but the very finest French champagnes.

With some ups and downs, California champagne has remained a favorite among wine consumers. A dip in the early 1970s was followed by increasing interest and sales. An extraordinarily available wine, champagne can be found at the low end of the scale for slightly over $2 to $12 and $14 at the top of the line. It is not a wine for holding over long periods of time. Properly stored, however, it will certainly enjoy a life of two years or more. Like all wines, it should be held in a cool, dark, vibration-free location at a nearly constant 55 to 65 degrees Fahrenheit, and abrupt changes of temperature, light, or humidity should be avoided.

When serving, champagne should be chilled to 31 to 41 degrees Fahrenheit, which may be achieved by placing the bottle in the refrigerator for two to four hours or placing it in a bucket of ice and water for about fifteen minutes. Over the years, as our knowledge and sophistication have increased, the saucer-bowl-type glass for champagne has fallen out of favor, and most restaurants today use a deep tulip or flute, which gives a long, steady flow of bubbles.

When opening the bottle, extreme care is essential. Many producers provide a warning on the label urging caution. The bottle should be held at an angle, pointing away from people or breakable objects. For complete safety, a bar towel or napkin should be draped over the cork to slow it down if it should fly out. After the wire hood has been loosened, the cork should be grasped in one hand, the bottle in the other. The cork is then slowly eased out by turning the *bottle.* Continue to hold the bottle at an angle, with a glass placed under the lip in case the champagne bubbles out. Pour each glass about one-half to one-third full.

Champagne, accepted throughout the world as a wine of celebration, is becoming more popular as a cocktail wine and almost traditional for

Sunday brunch. It comes in varying degrees of dryness — the most popular California champagnes are the brut and extra dry, though more and more wineries are showing an interest in producing drier champagnes, particularly of the blanc de noir style. California champagne is also available in pink as well as the usual white color.

With the range of choices available, there is sure to be a California champagne to satisfy almost any taste. Check the California Living Wine List by variety for champagne makers. Not all of the California champagne producers offer tasting of these special wines, and some who do, have a small tasting charge. The larger wineries in some regions offer tours, followed by tasting. It might be wise to call ahead so that you won't be disappointed. Often, for small tour groups, special arrangements can be made at California's champagne cellars throughout the state.

# California Brandy

"Everywhere grapes are grown for wine," begins a release from the California Brandy Advisory Board, "you also find brandy." The good reason for this is that everywhere grapes are grown for wine, something must be done with the grapes that aren't good enough for marketable wine. Something must also be done with the wines that aren't good enough to be marketable. And it is our good fortune that something wonderful is made from these grape and wine rejects. It is distilled wine, or brandy.

This is something of a rough assessment, as grapes are often grown specifically for brandy. In Cognac and Armagnac, for example, the ultimate product of the grape is brandy. But in California, a lot of brandy is made from what the industry refers to as "D.M.," distilling material, grapes and wine that are not marketable. And this is a fine, efficient arrangement. However, a good deal of brandy is also made from grapes grown specifically for that purpose, grapes such as Thompson Seedless, Tokay, Emperor, Grenache, and French Colombard (the grape of Cognac). None of these grapes makes an exceptional wine. In 1979, when October rains washed out a substantial portion of the Cabernet Sauvignon and Zinfandel in Napa and Sonoma Counties, many grapes were sold as distilling material. Perhaps an enterprising brandy maker will come out with varietal brandy as a result.

The brandy-making process begins by distilling wine and then adding purified water to the resulting high-proof liquid in order to reduce the percentage of alcohol. The brandy is then aged in oak casks for at least two years, and more usually, four.

That much of the process is the same wherever brandy is made. The differences between brandies come from the grapes used, the type of still used to distill the wine, the type of barrels used for aging, and whether the aged brandy is blended with caramel coloring, sweetening, or other flavoring and smoothing substances. The most highly-regarded brandies are made in pot stills out of sound grapes; they are aged in fine oak and unaltered so that their rich flavors are naturally derived from the grape, the distillation process, and the aging.

The pot still, which is widely used in the Cognac and Armagnac regions but seldom used in California, makes a heavier, stronger-flavored brandy than does the continuous-still process widely used in California and most of the rest of the world. In the pot still, one batch of wine is distilled at a time. This makes it difficult to separate the various elements of the distillate, according to the Brandy Advisory Board, and thus produces a heavier brandy. According to Alexis Lichine, in his *Encyclopedia of Wines and Spirits* (Knopf, 1967, $15.00), the pot-still method produces more of the higher alcohols, also called fusel oils, that add richness and complexity to a finished brandy. The continuous-still method uses a tall column through which, as the names implies, wine is piped. As steam is applied, the alcohol is stripped from the wine, producing the same high-proof liquid. Some of the better California brandies are blends of pot-still and continuous-still methods.

The combination of method and grapes used in California produce a lighter, fruitier sort of brandy than those traditionally associated with Cognac and Armagnac. But apparently, this lighter style is popular because California produces more than 98 percent of the American made brandy, and the state is responsible for more than 75 percent of the brandy consumed in the United States. "California brandy" has a legal definition; it must be made from grapes grown in California, and it must be aged in wood for at least two years. In practice, nearly all California brandies are aged at least four years, and some as long as ten, in American oak barrels charred on the inside. This charring produces the characteristic amber color of straight brandy, which is often enhanced with caramel coloring in blended brandies. Any benefits from aging, however, must come from the time in oak. Once the brandy is bottled, it does not improve. Keep a special bottle of fine brandy around for a special occasion, by all means, but don't expect it to improve as it waits. The better blended brandies are often marriages of those aged in wood for periods as long as twelve to fifteen years with younger brandies that still retain some of their natural fruitiness.

Only brandy made from wine can carry the simple legal designation "brandy," although brandies made from apples can be called "apple brandy" or "applejack." Brandies made from cherries can be called "cherry brandy," and so on. Fruit-flavored brandies are made by adding fruit flavoring to grape brandy. But when it's just "brandy," it's just from grapes.

Most California brandies are marketed at 80 proof or 40 percent alcohol. Some brandies go as high as 86 or 100 proof; the higher proofs are usually straight brandy, not blended with flavoring or smoothing agents and unsweetened. Here is a selection of some of the better brandies chosen from the more than three hundred on the market and the approximate suggested retail price per 750-milliliter bottle.

Almaden (Almaden Vineyards), $5.30.
Aristocrat (A. Perelli-Minetti Winery), $5.20.
California Gold (Windsor Vineyards), thirteen years old, $12.50.
Ceremony (Guild Wineries and Distilleries), five years old, $5.20.
Ceremony (Guild), eight years old, $6.30.
Christian Brothers (Christian Brothers Winery), $5.60.
Coronet (Schenley Distillers), $5.20.
Cresta Blanca (Guild Wineries and Distilleries), $5.44.
Cribari (Guild Wineries and Distilleries), $5.00.
E. & J. (Gallo), $5.20.
Hartley (United Vintners), $5.10.
Hiram Walker (Hiram Walker Distillery), $5.40.
Korbel (Korbel Winery), $5.70.
Lejon (United Vintners), $5.30.
Paul Masson (Paul Masson Vineyards), $5.20.
A. R. Morrow, 80 proof (A. Perelli-Minetti Winery), $5.20.
A. R. Morrow, 100 proof (A. Perelli-Minetti Winery), $7.50.
Old Mr. Boston (Glenmore Distillery), $5.10.
Parrott (Guild Wineries and Distilleries), $5.25.
Royal Host (East-Side Winery), $5.20.
Setrakian (California Growers Wineries), $5.30.
XO Rare Reserve (Christian Brothers), $9.00.

108/ Stocking a Wine Cellar

# Stocking a Wine Cellar

According to a Lyonnaise proverb, anyone who does not have two libraries in his home is lacking in either mind or spirit. One is, of course, made up of books. The other library is of wines. It is significant that the French do not call a home wine collection a cellar, a cave, or *chai,* as they do those of commercial wineries. It is called a *bibliotheque* or library, a collection to be used, perused, maintained, and enjoyed.

The size of a wine library is dictated by the space and money available as well as the owner's appetite for wine. A compact assortment of bottles in a corner of the coat closet may have little in common with an enclosed, air-conditioned, dehumidified, insulated room lined with racks containing thousands of bottles, but they both serve the same basic purposes. First, both offer a selection of suitable wines kept on hand for every occasion. In addition, buying wine when it is most available and storing it, gives the wine a chance to rest and improve in the bottle. Wines trundled home from the store, no matter how lovingly, then served the same night seldom show as well as those that have been given a few days to rest. Stored wine also increases in value. Wine that costs five dollars today may well be worth several times that in a few years, when the winery has sold out of it, and the wine is unavailable.

No matter what the recommendation, selecting wines to keep in a wine library is certainly a matter of personal taste. If with some experience, you find you drink much more red wine than white, vary your collection accordingly. When you find certain types of wine languishing in your cellar, buy less of them in the future and more of something you like better. For most people, however, an assortment that leans slightly toward red is ideal, because red wines tend to be held longer before they are consumed. Since the ideal is to have a variety of wines on hand to choose from, think in terms of wine types — dry whites, sweet whites, light reds, heavy reds, fortified wines — rather than specific varietals or brands.

The best way to select wines to cellar is by tasting as many as you can — at restaurants, at the homes of friends, at wine tastings, at wine shops that pour samples. Another way is to buy a bottle of something you are interested in, give it a few days to rest, then try it with dinner. If you like the wine, rush back to the store and buy some for your cellar. Then you will have it around whenever you want to match it with a meal. Buy what you like first, then consider what might be missing in your own library from the wide range of available wines.

The larger your cellar, of course, the greater variety of wines you can have and the more of each wine you can buy. A small collection of, say, three cases, must limit your purchases to a few bottles of each wine. Larger collections can be based on case lots. There is a good reason for buying wine in cases (twelve bottles in a case) — it's cheaper, as most stores and wineries give a 10 percent discount on purchases. But more important, you will be able to enjoy the wine over the course of several months, or even years in the case of red wines worth aging. If your space does not permit a large collection, try for as much variety as possible, but also try to buy at least two bottles of everything — and preferably three or four. Nothing is more frustrating than savoring a marvelous bottle of wine, knowing you have no more. Nothing is more soul satisfying than realizing, halfway through a bottle of superb Cabernet Sauvignon, that you have more bottles resting comfortably in the library, waiting patiently to please you again.

To provide something of a framework, the outlines of three sizes of wine cellar are offered: one holds 36 bottles (3 cases), one holds 150 bottles (12½ cases), and the largest holds 500 bottles (just under 42 cases). All the wines are California types, so you can choose from those selections listed elsewhere in this book. Note that as the cellars grow larger, they include a greater variety of wines, more of each wine (up to a case), and a larger percentage of age-worthy wines. The serious wine drinker can consume about a bottle a day, which means a thousand-bottle wine cellar would hold a three-year supply, give or take a few. Ideally, the thousand bottles would be divided among white and red wines for everyday drinking (about one-third), white and red wines that are ready to drink (about one-third) and wines, mostly reds but including some chosen whites, that have not yet reached their fullest maturity. Wines from the third group would then be shuffled into the second group as they mature. This can be done on a smaller scale too, but the thousand-bottle cellar seems ideal for the serious wine collector. Anything more is gilding the lily. Most of us, however, can get along splendidly with a few dozen cases, and can make do just fine with three or four, as in the following examples:

## A 36-Bottle Cellar
### White (18 bottles)

| | |
|---|---|
| 4 bottles | Generic white labeled White Wine, Table White, Chablis, or a simple varietal such as French Colombard, for everyday drinking. |
| 4 bottles | Chardonnay, for serving with rich dishes calling for a white wine. |
| 4 bottles | Sauvignon Blanc, for serving with light dishes calling for a white wine. |
| 4 bottles | Gewurztraminer, Chenin Blanc, or a light Johannisberg Riesling, for sipping before or between meals. |
| 2 bottles | Sweet white wines, such as late-harvest Rieslings, for enjoying after dinner on special occasions. |

### Red (18 bottles)

| | |
|---|---|
| 4 bottles | Generic red labeled Red Wine, Table Red, Burgundy, or a simple varietal such as Gamay, Gamay Beaujolais, or a light Zinfandel, for everyday drinking. |
| 4 bottles | Pinot Noir or a heavier Zinfandel, for serving with roast beef, roast chicken, or cheeses. |
| 2 bottles | Nonvintage Cabernet Sauvignon or Petite Sirah, for hearty dishes calling for a red wine with distinct flavor. |
| 6 bottles | Cabernet Sauvignon — the king of California red wines — for roast lamb, lamb chops, duck, game, and cheeses. |
| 2 bottles | Barbera or Charbono, for pasta and hearty dishes. |

## A 150-Bottle Cellar
### Dry White (4 cases)

| | |
|---|---|
| 1 case | Generic white labeled White Wine, Table Wine, or Chablis, or simple varietal such as French Colombard. |

| 1 case | Chardonnay, rich white wine. |
|--------|------------------------------|
| 1 case | Sauvignon Blanc, aromatic white wine. |
| 1 case | Dry or slightly off-dry Johannisberg Riesling, Gewurztraminer, or Chenin Blanc. |

## Red Wine (6½ cases)

| 1½ cases | Generic red labeled Red Wine, Table Wine, or Burgundy, or a simple varietal such as Gamay. |
|----------|---------------------------------------------------------------------------------------------|
| 6 bottles | Nonvintage Cabernet Sauvignon, Merlot, or Petite Sirah. |
| 2 cases | Cabernet Sauvignon. |
| 1 case | Pinot Noir. |
| 1½ cases | Rich Zinfandel, Barbera, or Charbono. |

## Sweet White and Sparkling Wine (1 case)

| 4 bottles | Sweet Johannisberg Riesling, Gewurztraminer, or Chenin Blanc, for after-dinner sipping. |
|-----------|-----------------------------------------------------------------------------------------|
| 2 bottles | Supersweet Riesling or other late-harvest wine. |
| 6 bottles | Brut (dry) sparkling wine. |

## Fortified Wine (1 case)

| 4 bottles | Dry Sherry. |
|-----------|-------------|
| 3 bottles | Sweet Sherry. |
| 3 bottles | Port. |
| 2 bottles | Angelica. |

## A 500-Bottle Cellar
### Dry White (13 cases)

| 3 cases | Generic white labeled White Wine, Table Wine, or Chablis, or a simple varietal such as French Colombard. |
|---------|---------------------------------------------------------------------------------------------------------|
| 5 cases | Chardonnays. |
| 2½ cases | Sauvignon Blancs. |
| 6 bottles | Pinot Blanc. |
| 1½ cases | Light dry or slightly off-dry Johannisberg Rieslings or Chenin Blancs. |
| 6 bottles | Dry or slightly off-dry Gewurztraminer. |

## Early-Drinking Red Wine (11 cases)

| | |
|---|---|
| 5 cases | Generic red labeled Red Wine, Table Wine or Burgundy, or simple varietals such as Gamay or Carignane. |
| 3 cases | Light-bodied Zinfandels or older fuller-bodied Zinfandels. |
| 1 case | Light-bodied Petite Sirahs or Pinot Noirs. |
| 2 cases | Nonvintage Cabernet Sauvignons or Merlots. |

## Age-Worthy Red Wine (12 cases)

| | |
|---|---|
| 5 cases | Cabernet Sauvignons. |
| 2 cases | Pinot Noirs. |
| 3 cases | Zinfandels. |
| 1 case | Petite Sirah. |
| 6 bottles | Merlot. |
| 6 bottles | Barbera or Charbono. |

## Sweet Wines and Sparkling Wines (5 cases plus 8 bottles)

| | |
|---|---|
| 1 case | Sparkling wines, especially dry (brut). |
| 2 cases | Sweet Johannisberg Rieslings (late-harvest style). |
| 6 bottles | Sweet Chenin Blanc or Gewurztraminer. |
| 4 bottles | Sweet Sauvignon Blanc or Semillon. |
| 6 bottles | Dry Sherry. |
| 4 bottles each | Sweet Sherry, Port, Angelica, and Moscato. |

# The Wineries of California

Whatever preconceived ideas you may have about how a winery should look, you will find a real-life version to match your fantasies somewhere in California. There are chateaux, some in replica of the fine chateaux of France. Other wineries have been set into redwood tanks, built inside hop kilns, barns, old gambling casinos, and dug into the side of hills. Some tunnel through rock, and others are located in the sterile boxlike structures of huge industrial complexes.

Many wineries are an individual's dream come true, with a little help from friends and neighbors at harvest time. A growing number are family affairs, second professions for doctors, lawyers, stockbrokers, oilmen, or members of the academic community. And, dotted all over the state are the huge corporate-owned or corporate-directed wineries, producing bottles in the millions.

The relative size of the winery does not give absolute indication of quality. A popular notion is that the loving care and personalized observation a wine can receive in the so-called boutique wineries makes for more delicate, flavorful, or extraordinary wines. But this is not necessarily a proven fact. As with the oft-repeated statement that there are no vintage years in California because every year is good, the corollary between small and quality is largely a myth.

In this book the state and the following list of wineries have been divided into Regions, A through E, as much for convenience as for any scientific reason. While it is recognized that one may speak in generalities about zones where, by virtue of soil and/or climate, certain grape varieties do extremely well or very poorly, there are also little pockets and microclimates throughout the state that tend to disprove any flat-out statement. Almost any experts on California viticulture, even those from other grape-growing regions of the world, support the statement that almost any grape variety, ancient or modern, can be grown somewhere in the state.

For the touring wine buff, the combination of fine growing areas, excellent teaching and research facilities at the universities and colleges, the inherent spirit of adventure in the industry, as well as the long traditions of quality and dedication are guarantees that every trip will bring new knowledge and excitement and the unending joy of discovery.

The listing that follows is as up to date as possible at the time of publication. The sure thing about California's wine industry is that it's not static. Every day new wineries are bonded, wines move from the barrel to the bottle, or volume increases enough to permit sales at the winery, and all of this takes place in an ever-increasing circle of distribution.

To help with quick decision making — where to taste, where to stop for a picnic, where to get a gift for Aunt Margaret — simple codings follow the names and addresses of the wineries.

> RS — retail sales
> G — gifts
> P — picnicking
> J — jug wines produced
> N — newsletter offered

You will find listings of the types of wines available in jugs as well as addresses and information about individual newsletters produced both by wineries and private individuals in later chapters on these subjects.

This book, like wine, is intended as a living thing that will change and improve over the years. Reader input would be invaluable, should you care to write with suggestions for additions or expansions.

# Napa County
## Region A

ALATERA VINEYARDS
5225 St. Helena Highway, Napa
94558
707-944-2914
4 miles north of Napa, 2 miles
south of Yountville

Tours by appointment only.

ALTA VINEYARD CELLAR
1311 Schramsberg Road, Calistoga 94515
707-942-6708

No tasting. Tours by appointment
only. First wine will be released
in fall 1980. RS

S. ANDERSON VINEYARD
1473 Yountville Crossroad, Napa
94558
707-252-8656

No tasting or tours. First wine will
be released in 1981.

BEAULIEU VINEYARD
1960 St. Helena Highway, Rutherford 94573
707-963-2411

Tasting daily 10–4. Tours every
hour. RS

BERINGER VINEYARDS
2000 Main St., St. Helena 94574
707-963-7115
Left off Highway 29, just north of
St. Helena

Tasting daily 9–4:30 in the pic-
turesque Rhine House. Tours
every 20 minutes include the
famous Beringer limestone cellar, 1,000 feet of tunnel, dug by
hand in the late 1800s. RS, G, J, N

BUEHLER VINEYARDS
820 Greenfield Road, St. Helena
94574
707-963-2155
No tasting or tours. RS

BURGESS CELLARS
1108 Deer Park Road, St. Helena
94574
707-963-4766
3.4 miles east from Highway 29

Tasting and tours by appointment
only. RS

CAKEBREAD CELLARS
P.O. Box 216, Rutherford 94573
707-963-9182 or 415-835-WINE
1 mile south of Rutherford on
Highway 29

Tasting and tours by appointment
only. Recommended time, 11
A.M., Saturday. RS, N

CASSAYRE-FORNI CELLARS
1271 Manley Lane, Rutherford
94573
707-944-2165
½ mile south of Rutherford off
Highway 29

Tasting and tours by appointment
only. Winery layout representative of old world chateau.
Cooperage housed in subterra-
nean cellar. Wines handpressed
in basket presses. RS, N

CAYMUS VINEYARDS
8700 Conn Creek Road, Rutherford 94573
707-963-4204 or 963-5683

Tasting and tours by appointment
only.

CHAPPELLET VINEYARD
1581 Sage Canyon Road, St. Helena 94574
707-963-7136

No tasting or tours. Sales to mailing list customers only.

CHARLES KRUG WINERY
2800 Main Street, St. Helena 94574
707-963-2761
Highway 29, just north of St. Helena

Tasting and tours daily 10–4. August Moon concerts scheduled each Saturday evening in August. RS, N

CHARLES F. SHAW VINEYARD AND WINERY
1010 Big Tree Road, St. Helena 94574
707-963-5459

Tours and retail sales by appointment only. RS

CHATEAU CHEVALIER WINERY
3101 Spring Mountain Road, St. Helena 94574
707-963-2342
2 miles northwest, Madrona and Spring Mountain Road

Tours by appointment only. Closed Sundays and holidays. A handsome, restored chateau with vineyards curving over surrounding hillsides. RS

CHATEAU MONTELENA
1429 Tubbs Lane, Calistoga 94515
707-942-5105

Tasting and tours by appointment only.

CHRISTIAN BROTHERS WINE AND CHAMPAGNE CELLARS (GREYSTONE)
2555 Main Street, St. Helena 94574
707-963-2719
¼ mile north of St. Helena on Highway 29

Tasting and tours daily 10–4. Large groups weekdays only, by appointment. Antique wine equipment and corkscrew collection on display. RS

CLOS DU VAL WINE COMPANY, LTD.
5330 Silverado Trail, Napa 94558
707-252-6711
5 miles north of Napa

No tasting. Tours by appointment only. RS

CONN CREEK WINERY
8711 Silverado Trail, St. Helena 94574
707-963-9100 or 963-3945
Intersection Highway 128 and Silverado Trail

Tasting, tours, and picnicking by appointment only. RS, P

CUVAISON WINERY
4550 Silverado Trail, Calistoga 94515
707-942-6266
6 miles north of St. Helena, just south of Dunaweal Lane

Tasting Thursday–Monday 10–4. Tours by appointment. RS, P

DEER PARK WINERY
1000 Deer Park Road, Deer Park 94576
707-963-5411

Tours by appointment only. First wines will be released fall 1980. RS

DIAMOND CREEK VINEYARDS
1500 Diamond Mountain Road, Calistoga 94515
707-942-6926

Eight tours scheduled each year with picnicking, swimming, boating, and barbecue for wine-oriented groups. Contact winery for information.

DOMAINE CHANDON
California Drive, Yountville 94599
707-944-2280 for visitor information; 707-944-2467 for restaurant

Exit Highway 29 at Yountville, go west on California Drive towards Veterans Home

Paid tasting, daily, May–October; Wednesday–Sunday, 11–6, November–April.

Tours approximately every hour. Champagne museum, model vineyard, duck pond. Restaurant on grounds. French cuisine. Lunch 11:30–2:30, prix fixe; dinner 6:00 on, a la carte. Reservations advised. Mardi Gras celebration. Bastille Day, free wine to all visitors. New Year's Eve party. Five minute walk from Greyhound stop in Yountville. RS, G, N

DUCKHORN WINERY
3027 Silverado Trail, St. Helena 94574
707-963-7108

1 mile north of St. Helena, corner Lodi Lane and Silverado Trail

Limited tasting by appointment only. Release of Napa Valley Merlot planned for fall 1980. Picnicking by reservation only. RS, P

FLORA SPRINGS WINE CO.
1978 West Zinfandel Lane, St. Helena 94574
707-963-5711

No tasting. Tours by appointment only. RS

FORMAN WINERY
2555 Madrona Avenue, St. Helena 94574
707-963-4613

Tours by appointment only. Retail sales of Merlot and Sauvignon Blanc will begin at winery in July 1980. RS

FRANCISCAN VINEYARDS
1178 Galleron Lane, St. Helena 94574
707-963-7111

1 mile north on Highway 29 at Galleron Road

Tasting and tours daily 10–5. RS, G

FREEMARK ABBEY WINERY
3022 St. Helena Highway North, St. Helena 94574
707-963-9694

1 mile north of St. Helena on Highway 29

Open for retail sales 9–4 daily. One tour each day at 2. Winery located in shopping complex. Restaurant serves lunch and dinner. RS, G

GRGICH HILLS CELLAR
1829 St. Helena Highway, Rutherford 94573
707-963-2784
2 miles north of Rutherford on Highway 29
Retail sales daily 10–4. Tours by appointment only. RS

HANNS KORNELL CHAMPAGNE CELLARS
P.O. Box 249, St. Helena 94574
707-963-2334
3 miles north of St. Helena on Highway 29, ¼ mile east on Larkmead Lane.
Tasting daily 10–4. RS, N

HEITZ WINE CELLARS
436 St. Helena Highway South, St. Helena 94574
707-963-3542
½ mile southeast on Highway 29
Tasting and retail sales weekdays only 11–4:30. RS

INGLENOOK VINEYARDS
1991 St. Helena Highway, Rutherford 94573
707-963-7184
Tasting daily 10:15–4:45. Tours every hour. No public picnic area, but will cater groups of 20–150 in former fermenting rooms or outdoors by prearrangement. Inglenook museum and wine library open to the public. RS, G, J, N

JOHN B. BECKETT CELLARS
1055 Atlas Peak Road, Napa 94558
707-452-4592 or 224-2022
Tasting and tours by appointment only.

JOHNSON TURNBULL VINEYARDS
8210 St. Helena Highway, Oakville 94562
707-963-5839
Not open to visitors at the present time.

JOSEPH PHELPS VINEYARDS
200 Taplin Road, St. Helena 94574
707-963-2745
Off Silverado Trail, 1 mile south of St. Helena
Retail sales, Monday–Friday, 8–5; Saturday 9–4. Tours by appointment only. Picnic grounds under construction. RS

LONG VINEYARDS
Box 50, St. Helena 94574
707-963-2496
Tours of small groups and retail sales by appointment only. First wines released are now sold out. Interested parties may write to be put on waiting list.

LOUIS M. MARTINI WINERY
254 South St. Helena Highway, St. Helena 94574
707-963-2736
1½ miles south of St. Helena on Highway 29
Tasting and tours daily 10–4:30. RS, G, J

MARKHAM WINERY
2812 North St. Helena Highway, St. Helena 94574
707-963-5292
Highway 29, 1¼ miles north of St. Helena
Tasting and tours daily, flexible schedule. RS

J. MATTHEWS NAPA VALLEY WINERY
1711 Main Street, Napa 94558
No phone listed.

Not open to visitors at the present time.

MAYACAMAS VINEYARDS
1155 Lokoya Road, Napa 94558
707-224-4030
Highway 29 north, left on Redwood Road west 4 miles, then 4 miles up Mt. Veeder to Lokoya

Retail sales and tours for groups smaller than 8 people, by appointment. RS, N

F. J. MILLER AND CO.
8329 St. Helena Highway, Napa 94558
707-963-4252

Tours by appointment only. F. Justin Miller, winemaker, will demonstrate Millerway Process of winemaking.

MONT LA SALLE VINEYARDS (CHRISTIAN BROTHERS)
4411 Redwood Road, Napa 94558
707-226-5566

Tasting 10–5. Tours 10–4:30. Gray Line bus tours scheduled regularly. RS, G

MT. VEEDER WINERY
1999 Mt. Veeder Road, Napa 94558
707-224-4039

Tours may be arranged, by appointment, for groups of fewer than six.

NAPA VINTNERS
1721-C Action Avenue, Napa 94558
707-255-9463

Tasting and retail sales by appointment. RS

NAPA WINE CELLARS
7481 St. Helena Highway, Oakville 94562
707-944-2565

Tasting and retail sales daily 11–5. RS

NICHELINI VINEYARD
2349 Lower Chiles Road, St. Helena 94574
707-963-3357
From Highway 29 at Rutherford, east 11 miles on Highway 128

Tasting and retail sales Saturday, Sunday 10–6. RS, P

POPE VALLEY WINERY
6613 Pope Valley Road, Pope Valley 94567
707-965-2192
Highway 29 to Deer Park Road, 12 miles east of St. Helena

Tasting and retail sales Saturday, Sunday, holidays 11–5; weekdays by appointment only. Informal tours. RS

RIVER BEND WINERY
8643 Silverado Trail, Rutherford 94576
707-963-7975

First wines to be released late 1980. No tasting or tours.

ROBERT KEENAN WINERY
3660 Spring Mountain Road, St. Helena 94574
707-963-9177
From Highway 29, 5 miles west on Spring Mountain Road.

Tours by appointment only.

ROBERT MONDAVI WINERY
7801 St. Helena Highway, Oakville 94558
707-963-9611
Highway 29, 12 miles north of Napa

Tasting and tours 10–5. Private catered lunches and dinners may be arranged by appointment. Regularly features art exhibits, Great Chefs of France Cooking Classes, and the annual Summer Festival of Jazz Greats. RS, G, J

ROBERT PECOTA WINERY
Box 571, Calistoga 94515
707-942-4627
.4 miles north on Bennett Lane

Tours by appointment only.

RODDIS CELLAR
1510 Diamond Mountain Road, Calistoga 94515
707-942-5868

Tasting and tours by appointment. First release will be Cabernet Sauvignon 1981. N

ROUND HILL CELLARS
1097 Lodi Lane, St. Helena 94574
707-963-5251
1 mile north of St. Helena on Lodi Lane

No tasting. Tours, informal or technical, by appointment. RS

RUTHERFORD HILL WINERY
P.O. Box 410, St. Helena 94574
707-963-9694
2 miles east of Rutherford on Silverado Trail

No tasting or tours except by appointment.

RUTHERFORD VINTNERS
1673 St. Helena Highway South, Rutherford 94573
707-963-4117
1 mile north of Rutherford on west side of Highway 29

Tasting daily 10–4:30, except major holidays. Tours by appointment. Picnic tables, by reservation for winery customers only. RS, G, P

V. SATTUI WINERY
White Lane, St. Helena 94574
707-963-7774
2 miles south on Highway 29 at White Lane

Tasting, informal tours daily 9:30–5:30. Deli and cheese shop. RS, G, P

ST. CLEMENT VINEYARDS
2867 St. Helena Highway North, St. Helena 94574
707-963-7221

Retail sales, in case lots, by appointment only. RS

SCHRAMSBERG VINEYARDS
Calistoga 94515
707-942-4558
5 miles north of St. Helena off Highway 29

Tours by appointment only. Produces only bottle-fermented champagnes. RS

SILVER OAK CELLARS
915 Oakville Crossroad, Oakville 94562
707-944-8866
1 mile east of Highway 29 at Oakville Crossroad

Tasting and tours by appointment only. Sale of Silver Oak Wines at Franciscan Winery. Only produces Cabernet Sauvignon. 1975 vintage to be released spring 1980.

SMITH-MADRONE VINEYARDS
4022 Spring Mountain Road, St. Helena 94574
707-963-2283

Visitors welcome but must phone ahead. Underground barrel aging cellar with sod roof. RS

SPRING MOUNTAIN VINEYARDS
2805 Spring Mountain Road, St. Helena 94574
707-963-4341
1 mile northwest, Madrona and Spring Mountain Roads

Tours by preappointment, 2:30 Monday–Friday. No tasting or retail sales.

STAG'S LEAP WINE CELLARS
5766 Silverado Trail, Napa 94558
707-944-2020
6 miles north of Napa

Tours each Friday, Saturday, Sunday. Retail sales 8–4. RS, P

STAG'S LEAP WINERY
6150 Silverado Trail, Napa 94558
707-253-1545

No tours, tasting, or retail sales.

STERLING VINEYARDS
1111 Dunaweal Lane, Calistoga 94515
707-942-5151
From Highway 29, 7 miles north of St. Helena, east ½ mile on Dunaweal Lane

Tasting daily 10:30–4:30, May 1 through October 31; Wednesday–Sunday only, November 1 through April 30. Self-guided tours. Tram fee: $3.00 16 years and older. For private tours, catered luncheons or prearranged dinners, call Special Events. RS, G, N

STONEGATE WINERY
1183 Dunaweal Lane, Calistoga 94515
707-942-6500
From Highway 29, 7 miles north of St. Helena, east on Dunaweal Lane

No tasting. Tours by appointment only. Retail and by-mail sales. Plans now being completed for picnic area and visitors' facilities. RS, N

SUTTER HOME WINERY, INC.
277 St. Helena Highway South, St. Helena 94574
707-963-3104
.3 miles south on Highway 29

Tasting and retail sales daily 10–4:30. RS

TREFETHEN VINEYARDS
1160 Oak Knoll Avenue, Napa 94558
707-255-7700
5 miles north of Napa on Highway 29

Tours by appointment only.

TULOCAY WINERY
1426 Coombsville Road, Napa 94558
707-255-4699
.9 miles east of Silverado Trail

No tasting. Tours by appointment only. RS

VILLA MT. EDEN WINERY
Oakville Crossroad, Oakville 94562
707-944-8431
North from Napa on Highway 29, 2 miles east of Oakville

Tasting by appointment only. No tours.

VOSE VINEYARDS
4035 Mt. Veeder Road, Napa 94558
707-944-2254

No tasting or tours.

YVERDON VINEYARDS
3787 Spring Mountain Road, St. Helena 94574
707-963-4270

No tasting or tours.

Z-D WINES
8383 Silverado Trail, Napa 94558
707-963-5188

Tasting and tours by appointment only. RS

## Solano County
Region A

CACHE CELLARS
Route 1, Box 2780, Davis 95616
916-756-6068
.3 mile south of Putah Creek on Pedrick Road, Davis. University airport 1 mile from winery.

Tasting by appointment only. RS

CADENASSO WINERY
1955 W. Texas Street, Fairfield 94553
707-425-5845

Off Highway 80 at Fairfield-Rio Vista exit

Tasting daily 8–6. RS

DIABLO VISTA WINERY
674 East H Street, Benicia 94510
415-837-1801

Tasting and tours by appointment only. Winery is located in cafeteria of old Yuba Manufacturing Complex. Many historic sites to visit in Benicia, the first capital of California. RS

WOODEN VALLEY WINERY
Route 1, Box 124, Suisun 94585
707-864-0730
4.5 miles northwest on Suisun Valley Road

Tasting daily 9–5. Closed Monday. No tours. RS

## Humboldt County
Region B

FIELDBROOK VALLEY WINERY
Fieldbrook Road, Fieldbrook 95521
707-839-4140

Tasting and tours by appointment only. Annual open house Oktoberfest for new releases. Extremely small production. Sells out of wine quickly. RS, N

WILLOW CREEK VINEYARDS
1904 Pickett Road, McKinleyville 95521
707-839-3373

Tasting and tours by appointment only. RS

WITTWER WINERY
2440 Frank Avenue, Eureka 95501
707-443-8852
No tasting or tours.

## Lake County
Region B

KONOCTI CELLARS
Thomas Lane, Finley 95451
707-279-8861
Highway 29, 3 miles north Kelseyville, 3 miles south of Lakeport

Tasting and sales will begin Spring 1980. Clear Lake State Park and Clear Lake resorts nearby. RS, P, J

LOWER LAKE WINERY
P.O. Box 950, Lower Lake 95457
707-994-4069
Highway 29, 1 mile south of Lower Lake

Tasting and tours Saturday, Sunday 10–5, or by appointment. RS

## Marin County
Region B

FAR NIENTE WINERY
200 Gate 5 Road, Sausalito 94965
415-332-0662
No tasting or tours.

GRAND PACIFIC VINEYARD CO.
134 Paul Drive, San Rafael 94903
415-479-WINE
From Highway 101, Smith Ranch Road exit to Northgate Industrial Park

Tasting by appointment only. No tours.

PACHECO RANCH WINERY
5495 Redwood Highway, Ignacio 94947
415-456-4099
No tasting or tours.

WOODBURY WINERY
32 Woodland Avenue, San Rafael 94901
415-454-2355

Tasting and tours by appointment only. Produces only vintage Port. RS

## Mendocino County
Region B

CRESTA BLANCA WINERY
2399 North State Street, Ukiah 95842
707-462-0565
Highway 101 to Lake Mendocino exit, right 1 mile to winery

Tasting and tours daily 9–5. RS, P, J

DACH VINEYARDS
9200 Highway 128, Philo 95466
707-895-3245

Winery not yet ready for visitors. Events in the area: Boonville Apple Fair, last weekend in September; Wool Growers Barbeque, spring.

EDMEADES VINEYARDS
5500 Highway 128, Philo 95466
707-895-3232
3 miles north of Philo

Tasting 10–6 (summer), 11–5 (winter). Tours by appointment only. Hendy Woods State Park and historic Mendocino only 30 minutes away. Wine judging at

Mendocino County Fair, Boonville, September. RS, P

FETZER VINEYARDS
1150 Bel Arbres Road, Redwood
Valley 95470
707-485-8998 or 485-8802

Tasting daily 9–5 at Hopland Tasting Room only. Winery tours by appointment only. Picnicking at winery and tasting room. Restaurant soon to be opened at Hopland Tasting Room. RS, G, P, J

HUSCH VINEYARDS
4900 Star Route, Philo 95466
707-895-3216 or 462-5370
5 miles northwest of Philo on
Highway 128

Tasting and tours by appointment. RS, P

LAZY CREEK VINEYARDS
4610 Highway 128, Philo 95466
707-895-3623

No tasting until 1981.

MCDOWELL VALLEY VINEYARDS
3811 Highway 175, Hopland
95449
707-744-1774 or 744-1053

Tours by appointment. No tasting or retail sales till spring 1980. Winery is designed to utilize solar energy. RS

MILANO WINERY
14594 South Highway 101, Hopland 95449
707-744-1396

Tasting and wine sales, Monday–Saturday 9–5. Tours by appointment. Winery is built

into an old hop kiln at the base of Duncan's Peak. A special tasting for the trade is conducted the last Friday and Saturday of May. RS, N

NAVARRO VINEYARDS
5601 Highway 128, Philo 95466
707-895-3686
3 miles north of Philo

Tasting Friday–Monday 10–6. Tours by appointment. Close to Hendy Woods State Park. RS, P, J

PARDUCCI WINE CELLARS
501 Parducci Road, Ukiah 95482
707-462-3828
2 miles north on Highway 101, right on Lake Mendocino Drive, left on Parducci Road

Tasting daily 9–6 (summer), 9–5:30 (winter). Tours on the hour. Exhibits by local artists. RS, G, P, J

PARSONS CREEK WINERY
3001 South State Street, #4, Ukiah 95482
707-462-8900

No tasting or tours. White varietal wines only, field-crushed and pressed.

TYLAND VINEYARDS
2200 McNab Ranch Road, Ukiah
95482
707-462-1810

Tasting weekends only, or by appointment. Tours by appointment. Hiking permitted. RS, G, P

WEIBEL CHAMPAGNE VINEYARDS
7051 North State Street, Redwood
Valley 95470

707-485-0321

North of Highway 20 off Highway 101

Tasting daily 9–6. No tours. Tasting center serves as locale for various community art and social events. RS, G, P

## Sonoma County Region B

ALEXANDER VALLEY VINEYARDS
8644 Highway 128, Healdsburg 95448
707-433-7209
8 miles east of Healdsburg

Tasting, informal tours, and retail sales 10–5, weekdays; weekends 12–5. Winery on site of ranch of Alexander family for whom the valley is named. Many historical features. RS, P, N

BALVERNE WINE CELLARS
10810 Hillview Road, Windsor 95492
707-433-6913

Not yet ready for visitors.

BANDIERA WINES
155 Cherry Creek Road, Cloverdale 95425
707-894-2352
Highway 101 at Cloverdale Boulevard, 2 blocks west

Retail sales daily 1–6. Tours. Wine museum of antique winery equipment. RS

BUENA VISTA WINERY, INC.
18000 Old Winery Road, Sonoma 95476
707-938-1266

End of Old Winery Road, 1 mile east of Sonoma

Tasting daily 10–5. Self-guided tours. Winery is on the site of the winery founded by Count Agoston Haraszthy, father of the California wine industry. RS, G, P, N

CAMBIASO VINEYARDS
1141 Grant Avenue, Healdsburg 95448
707-433-5508
Healdsburg Avenue offramp, east on Grant Avenue

No tasting. Tours by appointment only. RS, J

CECIL DE LOACH VINEYARDS
1791 Olivet Road, Santa Rosa 95401
707-526-9111

No tours or tasting. Interested parties should call winery.

CHATEAU ST. JEAN
8555 Sonoma Highway, Kenwood 95452
707-833-4134
Highway 12, 8 miles east of Santa Rosa

Tasting daily 10–4:30. Tours by appointment only. RS, P

LA CREMA VINERA
1250 Holm Road, Petaluma 94952
707-762-0393

No tasting. Retails or tours by appointment only. First wines will be released in summer of 1980.

DAVIS BYNUM WINERY
8075 Westside Road, Healdsburg 95448

707-433-5852

Westside Road west from Healdsburg, 8 miles

Tasting daily 9–5. Tours by appointment only. RS

DRY CREEK VINEYARD
3770 Lambert Bridge Road
Healdsburg, 95448
707-433-1000
Corner Dry Creek and Lambert Bridge Roads

Tasting daily 10:30–4:30. Tours by appointment. Open house with music, usually scheduled first Saturday in February, May, September, December. Half a mile from Healdsburg airport. Will pick up by prior arrangement. RS, P

FENTON ACRES WINERY
6192 Westside Road, Healdsburg
707-433-2305

No tasting or tours.

FIELD STONE WINERY
10075 Highway 128, Healdsburg 95448
707-433-7266

Winery open daily 9–5, except on major holidays. Informal tours. No tasting. Winery is unique *chai* construction. RS, P

FOPPIANO WINE COMPANY
12707 Old Redwood Highway, Healdsburg 95448
707-433-7272
2 miles south of Healdsburg, west of Highway 101 at Healdsburg Avenue exit

Tasting daily 10–4:30. Tours by appointment. RS, P, J

GEYSER PEAK WINERY
P.O. Box 25, Geyserville 95441
707-433-6585
West at Canyon Road exit from Highway 101, at Geyserville

Tasting daily 10–5. Tours on request, as staff permits. Two walking trails. Summer musical events. Giant lighted Christmas tree. RS, P, G, J, N

GRAND CRU VINEYARDS
1 Vintage Lane, Glen Ellen 95442
707-996-8100
Highway 12, Dunbar Road exit 2 miles north of Glen Ellen, west on Henno

Tasting Saturday, Sunday, holidays 10–5. Retail sales Monday–Friday 8–5; Saturday, Sunday 10–5. Tours by appointment. Jack London State Park one mile to south. RS, P, N

GUNDLACH-BUNDSCHU WINERY
3775 Thornsberry Road, Sonoma 95476
707-938-5277
From Sonoma Plaza go east on Napa Street to Old Winery Road, turn left. Right on Lovall Valley Road. Right on Thornsberry

Tasting and tours, Friday, Saturday, Sunday 12–4:30. RS, P

HACIENDA WINE CELLARS
1000 Vineyard Road, Sonoma 95476
707-938-3220
1.5 miles northeast of Sonoma Plaza

Tasting daily 10–5. Tours by appointment. Vineyards surrounding winery were established by Count Agoston Haraszthy in 1892. RS, G, P, N

HANZELL VINEYARDS
18596 Lomita Avenue, Sonoma 95476
707-996-3860

No tasting. Tours and retail sales by appointment.

J. J. HARASZTHY & SON
14301 Arnold Drive, Glen Ellen 95442
707-996-3040
½ mile south of Glen Ellen

No tasting. By appointment only.

HOP KILN WINERY
6050 Westside Road, Healdsburg 95448
707-433-6491
6½ miles southwest of Healdsburg

Tasting and sales, daily 10–5. Group tours by appointment. Winery patrons may picnic in meadow overlooking vineyards. Winery has been designated a California Historical Landmark. Original hop drying towers now house winery and tasting room. RS, P, N

HORIZON WINERY
2594 Athena Court, Santa Rosa 95401
707-544-7961

No tours. Produces only Zinfandel. Will deliver by prior arrangement.

IRON HORSE VINEYARDS
9786 Ross Station Road, Sebastopol 95472
707-887-2913

Tasting by appointment only.

ITALIAN SWISS COLONY WINERY
Asti, 95413
707-894-2280

Tasting and tours daily 9–5. Deli. RS, G, P, J

JOHNSON'S ALEXANDER VALLEY WINERY
8333 Highway 128, Healdsburg 95448
707-433-2319

Tasting daily 10–5, except major holidays. Theatre pipe organ in winery. Concerts monthly. Various musical events during summer. Will pick up visitors at Healdsburg airport, by prior arrangement. RS, P, N, J

JORDAN VINEYARD AND WINERY
1474 Alexander Valley Road, Healdsburg 95448
707-433-6955

No tasting or tours.

KENWOOD VINEYARDS
9592 Sonoma Highway, Kenwood 95452
707-833-5891

Tasting and retail sales daily 9–5. Tours by appointment only. RS

KISTLER VINEYARDS
2995 Nelligan Road, Glen Ellen 95442
707-833-4662

Winery is not open to the public. Wine sales by mail only.

KORBEL CHAMPAGNE CELLARS
13250 River Road, Guerneville 95446
707-887-2294

Tasting in opulent tasting room, former brandy warehouse, daily 9–4:30. Tours: Summer — 9:45–3:45, every 45 minutes; Winter — 10–3, every hour. Annual Margot Doss spring walk. Historic rail station, brandy tower, and aging cellars. RS, G, P

LAMBERT BRIDGE
4085 West Dry Creek Road, Healdsburg 95448
707-433-5855

Call for appointment to visit.

LANDMARK VINEYARDS
9150 Los Amigos Road, Windsor 95492
707-838-9466
Highway 101 north of Santa Rosa

Tasting and informal tours, weekends, 10–5, or by appointment. RS, P

LYTTON SPRINGS WINERY, INC.
750 Lytton Springs Road, Healdsburg 95448
707-433-7721
From Highway 101, 1 mile west on Lytton Springs Road

Tasting, Monday–Friday 9–5. Tours by appointment. Produces only Zinfandel. RS, N

MARK WEST VINEYARDS
7000 Trenton-Healdsburg Road, Forestville 95436
707-544-4813
Highway 101 north of Santa Rosa to River Road, 5½ miles west to Trenton-Healdsburg Road

Tours and retail sales by appointment only. RS, P

MARTINI & PRATI WINES, INC.
2191 Laguna Road, Santa Rosa 95401
707-823-2404
Highway 101 to Guerneville Road, 8.1 miles northwest on Laguna Road

Tasting Monday–Friday, 9–12, 1–4. No tours. RS, J

MATANZAS CREEK WINERY
6097 Bennett Valley Road, Santa Rosa 95404
707-542-8242

Tasting by invitation to mailing list customers only. Tours and retail sales by appointment only.

MILL CREEK VINEYARDS
1401 Westside Road, Healdsburg 95448
707-433-5098
1 mile west of Healdsburg

Retail sales only 10–4:30, daily. RS

NERVO WINERY
19585 Geyserville Ave., Geyserville 95441
707-857-3417
Independence Lane exit, 4 miles north of Healdsburg off Highway 101

Tasting daily 10–5. Old winery equipment displayed. Case sales on holidays throughout the year. RS, P, J, N

PASTORI WINERY
23189 Geyserville Ave., Cloverdale 95425
707-857-3418
Canyon Road exit to Geyserville Avenue, 1 mile north

Tasting and retail sales daily 9–5. RS

J. PEDRONCELLI WINERY
1220 Canyon Road, Geyserville 95441
707-857-3619
Canyon Road exit from Highway 101, 1 mile west

Tasting and retail sales daily 10–5. Tours by appointment. RS, J

A. RAFANELLI WINERY
4685 West Dry Creek Road, Healdsburg 95448
707-433-1385
3½ miles northwest, Dry Creek Road exit from Highway 101

No tasting. Tours by appointment only. Wines sold only by the case.

RIVER ROAD VINEYARDS
7145 River Road, Forestville 95436
707-887-7890

No tasting or tours.

ROBERT STEMMLER WINERY
3805 Lambert Bridge Road, Healdsburg 95448
707-433-6334
3.4 miles northwest on Lambert Bridge Road off Highway 101

Tasting by appointment only. RS

RUSSIAN RIVER VINEYARDS
5700 Gravenstein Highway North, Forestville 95436
707-887-1562

Tasting room to open spring 1980. Tours by appointment only. Restaurant with garden patio. RS, G

SAUSAL WINERY
7370 Highway 128, Healdsburg 95448
707-433-2285

Open for tours by appointment only. No tasting.

SEBASTIANI VINEYARDS
389 Fourth Street East, Sonoma 95476
707-938-5532

Tasting and retail sales 10–5 daily. Tours every 20 minutes. Old and intricately carved casks and woodwork throughout winery. Historic Sonoma Plaza within walking distance. Gamay Beaujolais Nouveau celebration, November 15 annually. RS, J, N

SHILO VINEYARDS
8075 Martinelli Road, Forestville 95436
707-887-2176

No tasting, tours, or retail sales. First release will be late 1980.

SIMI WINERY
16275 Healdsburg Avenue, Healdsburg 95448
707-433-6981

Tasting daily 10–5. Tours at 11, 1, 3. RS, G, P, N

SONOMA VINEYARDS
11455 Old Redwood Highway, Healdsburg 95448
707-433-6511

Tasting daily 10–5. Tours on the hour. Additional tasting and sales rooms located in Tiburon and on Union Street in San Francisco. RS, G, P, N

SOTOYOME WINERY
641 Limerick Lane, Healdsburg
95448
707-433-2001
1½ miles south of Healdsburg off
Old Redwood Highway

Tasting by appointment only.

SOUVERAIN CELLARS
P.O. Box 528, Geyserville 95441
707-433-6918
From Highway 101, Independence
Lane offramp, west

Tasting, daily 10–5:30. Tours
hourly 10–4. Bike and riding
trails lead to winery. Restaurant in winery open daily for
lunch 1–3; dinner Wednes-
day–Sunday 5–9. English
Christmas Feast, weekends
prior to Christmas. Hollyberry
Faire, November, and Summer
Arts Festival. RS, G, J, N

TRENTADUE WINERY
19170 Redwood Highway, Geyserville 95441
707-433-3104
4 miles north of Healdsburg, Independence Lane offramp from
Highway 101

Tasting and retail sales daily
10–5. Tours on request. RS, G, P

VALLEY OF THE MOON WINERY
751 Madrone Road, Glen Ellen
95442
707-996-6601

Tasting and retail sales daily except Thursday, 10–5. RS

VIEWS LAND CO. VINEYARDS AND
WINERY
18701 Gehricke Road, Sonoma
95476
707-938-3768
Not open to the public.

VINA VISTA VINEYARDS
Chianti Road, Geyserville 95441
415-969-3160
Canyon Road exit from Highway
101, 1.9 miles north on Chianti
Road

Tasting and tours by appointment
only.

WILLOWSIDE VINEYARDS
3349 Industrial Drive, Santa Rosa
95401
707-528-1599 or 544-7504

Visits by appointment only, but
owners happy to give tours to
interested wine buffs.

## Alameda County
Region C

CONCANNON VINEYARD
4590 Tesla Road, Livermore 94550
415-447-3760
From Highway 580, south on
Vasco 3 miles to Telsa Road,
turn right.

Tasting Monday–Saturday 9–4;
Sunday 12–4:30. Tours Mon-
day–Friday 9, 10, 11, 1, 2, 3.
Saturday, Sunday 12, 1, 2, 3.
Picnic tables available by ad-
vance reservation. Special
events: Art in the Vineyard,
Sunday, Memorial Day Week-

end; Tasting from the Wood, Thanksgiving Weekend; White Wine Preview Tasting, President's Holiday Weekend. No buses. RS, G, P, N

FRETTER WINE CELLARS
805 Camelia Street, Berkeley 94710
415-525-3232

Retail sales only. RS

LIVERMORE VALLEY CELLARS
1508 Wetmore Road, Livermore 94550
415-447-1751

Tasting and tours by appointment only.

LLORDS & ELWOOD WINERY — *See Santa Clara listing.*

MONTCLAIR WINERY
910 81st Avenue, Oakland 94621
415-658-1014

No tasting or tours. N

J. W. MORRIS PORT WORKS
1215 Park Avenue, Emeryville 94608
415-655-3009

No tasting, tours by appointment only. An open house is conducted two or three times a year. Write to be placed on mailing list. RS

NUMANO SAKE COMPANY
708 Addison Street, Berkeley 94710
415-548-0226

Tasting daily 11–5. Tours by appointment. AC Transit Bus #51 stops one block from location. RS, G, N

OAK BARREL WINERY
1201 University Avenue, Berkeley 94702
415-849-0400
One block east of San Pablo Avenue

Tasting limited; no tours. Winecraft supplies for home winemaking and wineries. RS, J

RICHARD CAREY WINERY
1695 Martinez Street, San Leandro 94577
415-352-5425
Off Davis Street, directly across from San Leandro BART station

Tasting tours, Friday and Saturday 11–4. RS, J

STONY RIDGE WINERY
1188 Vineyard Avenue, Pleasanton 94566
415-846-2133
From Highway 680 to Sunol Boulevard towards Pleasanton to Vineyard Avenue

Tasting Monday–Friday 12–5, Saturday, Sunday 11–5. Tours by appointment only. A second tasting room is open at 301 Capitola Avenue, Capitola, CA 95010. RS, J

VEEDERCREST VINEYARD
1401 Stanford Avenue, Emeryville 94608
415-652-3103
100 yards southwest of corner of Hollis and Stanford

Tasting by appointment only. No tours.

VILLA ARMANDO WINERY
553 St. John Street, Pleasanton 94566
415-846-5488
Tasting and tours daily 12–5:30. Restaurant on premises open Wednesday–Sunday. RS, G

WEIBEL CHAMPAGNE VINEYARDS
1250 Stanford Avenue, Mission San Jose 94538
415-656-2340
1.1 miles south from Highway 680, ½ mile left on private road
Tasting daily 10–5. Tours Monday–Friday 10–3. RS, G, P

WENTE BROS. WINERY
5565 Tesla Road, Livermore 94550
415-447-3603
From Highway 580, south on Vasco, 3 miles to Tesla Road, turn right
Tasting Monday–Saturday 9–4:30. Sunday 11–4:30. Tours Monday–Friday 10–3:30.
Picnicking by reservation. RS, G, P, N

## Contra Costa County
Region C

CONRAD VIANO WINERY
150 Morello Avenue, Martinez 94553
415-228-6465
1 mile east of VA Hospital on Highway 4, 1 mile north of Morello Avenue
Tasting daily 9–12.

J. E. DIGARDI WINERY
P.O. Box 88, Martinez 94554
415-228-2638
2.3 miles southeast on Pacheco Boulevard
Tasting and tours by appointment only.

## Monterey County
Region C

JEKEL VINEYARD
40155 Walnut Avenue, Greenfield 93927
408-674-5522
1 mile west of Highway 101, Walnut offramp
Tasting and tours daily 11–5. Winery set in center of vineyard. RS, G

MONTEREY PENINSULA WINERY
2999 Monterey-Salinas Highway, Monterey 93940
408-372-4949
Tasting daily 10–Sundown. Tours when guide available. Annual grape stomp, first Saturday in October. Gift items and tasting at Gifts from Bacchus, 7th and Dolores, Carmel. RS, G, P, J, N

THE MONTEREY VINEYARD
800 South Alta Street, Gonzales 93926
408-675-2326
Highway 101 at south edge of Gonzales
Tasting and tours daily 10–5. Large groups, please call in advance. RS, G, N

VENTANA VINEYARDS WINERY
P.O. Box G, Los Coches Road, Soledad 93960
408-678-2306
5.8 miles southwest of Soledad, take Arroyo Seco from 101, 3 miles left at Los Coches Road

Winery conducts an annual spring tasting of new wines. Other tasting and tours by appointment only. RS, N

## San Benito County
Region C

CALERA WINE COMPANY
11300 Cienega Road, Hollister 95023
408-637-9170
11 miles south of Hollister

No tasting. Tours Saturday at 11. Call Friday for reservation. Pinnacles National Monument, 18 miles south. Fremont Peak State Park, 15 miles north. RS

## San Luis Obispo County
Region C

ESTRELLA RIVER WINERY
Shandon Star Route, Highway 46, Paso Robles 93446
805-238-6300
6 miles east of Paso Robles on Highway 46
Paso Robles airport, 3 miles west

Tasting and tours daily 10–4. RS, G, P

HOFFMAN MOUNTAIN RANCH VINEYARDS
Adelaida Road, Star Route, Paso Robles 93446
805-238-4945

Tasting, sales, and gift shop at tasting room at Black Oak Corner, Paso Robles, just west of Highway 101 on 24th Street. Tours of winery by appointment only. Mozart Festival Art Show and Wine Tasting in April. RS, G, N

LAWRENCE WINERY
P.O. Box 698, San Luis Obispo 93406
805-544-5800
1.2 miles southeast on Corbett Canyon Road from Highway 227

Tasting and tours, Monday–Saturday, 10–4; Sunday 12–4. RS, G, P, J

MASTANTUONO WINERY
101¾ Willow Creek Road, Paso Robles 93446
805-238-1078

Retail sales and tours by appointment. RS

PESENTI WINERY
2900 Vineyard Drive, Templeton 93465
805-434-1030
3 miles west of Highway 101 on Vineyard Drive

Tasting and self-conducted tours, Monday–Saturday 8–6, Sunday 9–6. RS, G, J

RANCHITA OAKS WINERY
9351 Yolanda Avenue, Northridge 91324
213-993-9695

Winery is not open to public. Sales by mailing list only.

LAS TABLAS WINERY
Winery Road, Templeton 93465
805-434-1389
3 miles west of Highway 101

Tasting, retail sales, and gift shop open Monday–Saturday 9–6; Sundays and holidays 10–5. RS, G

YORK MOUNTAIN WINERY
York Mountain Road, Templeton 93465
805-238-3925
Off Highway 46, 9 miles west of Highway 101

Tasting and retail sales daily 10–5. Tours by appointment only. RS, G

# San Mateo County
Region C

OBESTER WINERY
12341 Highway 92, Half Moon Bay 94019
415-726-WINE
1 mile east of Half Moon Bay

Tasting, tours, and retail sales Saturday, Sunday 10–5. Large groups, please call for appointment. RS, P

WOODSIDE VINEYARDS
340 Kings Mountain Road, Woodside 94061
415-851-7475
1.4 miles west of Woodside

Tasting Saturday, Sunday by appointment. RS

# Santa Barbara County
Region C

BALLARD CANYON WINERY
1825 Ballard Canyon Road, Solvang 95463
805-688-7585
Tasting and tours by appointment only.

J. CAREY CELLARS
1711 Alamo Pintado Road, Solvang 93463
805-688-8554
2 miles north of Highway 246

Tasting and tours daily 10–4 (June through August); by appointment (September through May). Winery is in old barn. RS, P

FIRESTONE VINEYARD
P.O. Box 244, Los Olivos 93441
805-688-3940
½ mile north of junction Highway 154 and Highway 101

Tours and tasting Monday–Saturday 10–4. RS

RANCHO SISQUOC WINERY
Route 1, Box 147, Santa Maria 93454
805-937-3616
18 miles east of Santa Maria on Foxen Canyon Road

Tasting and retail sales Monday–Saturday, 9–5. Tours and picnic privileges by prior arrangement. Los Padres National Forest nearby. RS, P

SANTA BARBARA WINERY
202 Anacapa Street, Santa Barbara 93101
805-963-8924 or 962-3812
1 block east of State Street, two blocks north of ocean

Tasting and self-guided tours, daily 10–5. Group tours by appointment. RS

SANTA YNEZ VALLEY WINERY
365 Refugio Road, Santa Ynez 93460
805-688-8381
1 mile south of Highway 246

Tasting and tours, weekdays by appointment; Saturday 10–4. Planning to open Sunday. Open house every spring with tasting, food, and music. Ask to be placed on mailing list. RS

VEGA VINEYARDS WINERY
9496 Santa Rosa Road, Buellton 93427
805-688-2415

Tasting and sales, weekends only. RS

ZACA MESA WINERY
Foxen Canyon Road, Los Olivos 93441
805-688-3310
From 101 Zaca Station Road, turn right, 9 miles on right

Tasting and tours, daily 10–4. RS, P, N

# Santa Clara County
Region C

ALMADEN VINEYARDS
1530 Blossom Hill Road, San Jose 95118
408-433-1312

From the north, Highway 101 or Highway 280 to Highway 17, exit at Los Gatos-Santa Cruz. Continue to Camden Avenue exit, left 4 miles to Blossom Hill Road exit to Highway 82, ½ mile to Blossom Hill exit, 1 mile west to winery

Tours only 10–3, Monday–Friday. Tasting at Don Pacheco Tasting Gardens, 8090 Pacheco Pass Road, Hollister (San Benito County).

ANGELO C. BERTERO WINERY
3920 Hecker Pass Highway, Gilroy 95020
408-842-3032
From Highway 101, 4 miles west on Highway 152

Tasting and tours daily 9–5. Live oak tree estimated to be 400 years old on picnic site. RS, G, P

CASA DE FRUTA
6680 Pacheco Pass Highway, Hollister 95023
408-637-0051
14 miles east of Gilroy on Highway 152

Tasting, retail sales, fruit and gift shop open daily 8–8 (summer), 9–6 (winter). Weekday picnicking, no charge. Summer weekends, picnicking restricted to day-use park, nominal charge. Two lakes, animal zoo, restaurant, and overnight facilities adjacent. Produces fruit and berry wines. RS, G, P

CONGRESS SPRINGS VINEYARDS
23600 Congress Springs Road, Saratoga 95070
408-867-1409
3.5 miles from Saratoga on Highway 9

Tasting and tours by appointment. Public prerelease tasting Memorial Day weekend. RS, P, N

EMILIO GUGLIELMO WINERY, INC.
1480 East Main Avenue, Morgan Hill 95037
408-779-2145
1.5 miles east on Main Avenue from Monterey Street (El Camino Real)

Tours by appointment only.

FORTINO WINERY
4525 Hecker Pass Highway, Gilroy 95020
408-842-3305
From Highway 101, Watsonville Road at Morgan Hill to Hecker Pass Highway, 5 miles west of Highway 152

Tasting and tours daily 9–6. RS, P

GEMELLO WINERY, INC.
2203 El Camino Real, Mountain View 94040
415-948-7723
.8 mile south of San Antonio Road

Tasting Saturday only 12–4. Tours by appointment. Retail sales daily 9–9. RS

A. GIURLANI & BROS. INC.
1266 Kifer Road, Sunnyvale 94086
408-738-0220
Winery makes only vinegar.

HECKER PASS WINERY
4605 Hecker Pass Highway, Gilroy 95020
408-842-8755
5 miles west of Gilroy

Tasting daily 9–5. Tours by appointment. Spring Wine Festival in April; Fall Harvest Festival in October. RS

KATHRYN KENNEDY WINERY
13180 Pierce Road, Saratoga 95070
408-867-4170

Produces only Cabernet Sauvignon. No wines available until 1982.

KIRIGIN CELLARS
11550 Watsonville Road, Gilroy 95020
408-847-8827
5 miles southwest on Watsonville Road

Tasting and tours daily 9–6. Summer concert. RS, G, P, N

LIVE OAKS WINERY
3875 Hecker Pass Highway, Gilroy 95020
408-842-2401
From Highway 101 west on first street 4.5 miles

Tasting daily 8–5. Close to Mt. Madonna Park. RS, P, J

LLORDS & ELWOOD WINERY
12 North 25th Street, San Jose 95116
213-553-2368
For tours or tasting, contact Los Angeles office.

MARTIN RAYWINERY
22000 Mt. Eden Road, Saratoga 95070
415-321-6489

No tasting. Tours by appointment only. Call for directions. RS

MIRASSOU VINEYARDS
3000 Aborn Road, San Jose 95135
408-274-4000
Capitol Expressway, east from Highway 101, turn right on Aborn Road, 2 miles

Tasting Monday–Saturday 10–5, Sunday 12–4. Tours, approximately 10:30, 12, 2:30, 4. Large groups, call first. In 1980: Vintage Festival September 6/7, Saturday 12–5, Sunday 12–4, $1.50 fee. RS, G, N

MT. EDEN VINEYARDS
22020 Mt. Eden Road, Saratoga 95070
408-867-5783

Tours by appointment only. Limited retail sales. Call for directions. RS

NOVITIATE WINES
300 College Avenue, Los Gatos 95030
408-354-6471
Highway 17 to east, Los Gatos turnoff, turn right on Los Gatos Boulevard, turn left at College Avenue to Prospect Avenue, turn right into Jesuit Center

Tasting Monday–Saturday 9–4. Closed Sundays, legal, and religious holidays. Tours Monday–Friday 1:30, 2:30; Saturday 10, 11. Outdoor site for dinners, available by group reservation, April to October, Thursday, Friday, and Saturday nights. RS, G

PAGE MILL WINERY
13686 Page Mill Road, Los Altos Hills 94022
415-948-0958
.7 mile west of Highway 280

Tasting and tours by appointment only. RS

PAUL MASSON VINEYARDS
13150 Saratoga Avenue, Saratoga 95070
408-257-7800
From Highway 280, 3 miles southwest on Saratoga Avenue

Tasting and self-guided tours daily 10–4, except major holidays. Special events: Musica at the Vineyards (classical); Vintage Sounds (jazz/folk); Merola opera; Shakespeare; chess tournament. Special events information: 408-257-4753. Lunch or dinner at nearby Mountain Winery by prearrangement (6 months in advance), summer only. RS, G, J, N

PEDRIZZETTI WINERY
1645 San Pedro Avenue, Morgan Hill 95037
408-779-7380
1.5 miles from Highway 101

Tasting daily 9:30–6. Tours by appointment only. Retail sales at 19200 Monterey Road. Picnic area at winery now being planned. Winery is just a five minute drive from Henry Coe State Park. RS, G, J

PENDLETON WINERY
2156G O'Toole Avenue, San Jose 95131
408-280-1300 or 946-1303
No further information supplied.

LA PURISIMA WINERY
725 Sunnyvale-Saratoga Road, Sunnyvale 94087
408-738-1011
From Highway 85, 2 miles east on El Camino Real

Tasting Tuesday–Friday 11–2 and 4:30–6:30. Weekends 11–6. Group tours by appointment. RS

RAPAZZINI WINERY
4350 North Monterey Highway, Gilroy 95020
408-842-5649
3 miles south of Gilroy on Highway 101

Tasting, retail sales, and gift shop daily 9–5. Earth Walk, following the San Andreas Fault line and viewing the new seismograph exhibit. Additional tasting rooms: 11 Franklin Street, across from Mission San Juan Bautista; and 6th and Mission Streets, Carmel. RS, G, P

RICHERT & SONS WINERY
1840 West Edmundson Avenue, Morgan Hill 95037
408-779-5100
Tasting by appointment only. RS

RIDGE VINEYARDS, INC.
17100 Monte Bello Road, Cupertino 95014
408-867-3233

4.4 miles from Stevens Creek Reservoir
Tasting Saturday 11–3. RS

RONALD LAMB WINERY
17785 Casa Lane, Morgan Hill 95037
408-779-4268
Tasting weekends only, by appointment.

SAN MARTIN WINERY
13000 Depot Street, San Martin 95046
408-683-4000
Tasting, retail sales, and gift shop daily 9:30–5:30. Tasting rooms in Morgan Hill, Gilroy, and Solvang. RS, G, P, J, N

SARAH'S VINEYARD
4005 Hecker Pass Highway, Gilroy 95020
408-842-4278
Tasting Saturday, Sunday 12–4. During the week, phone for appointment to tour or taste. Walking trails to nearby Uvas Creek. RS, P

SHERRILL CELLARS
1185 Skyline Boulevard, Palo Alto 94062
415-941-6023 or 851-1932
1 mile south of Alpine intersection
Tasting and tours by invitation, bi-monthly. Call winery for times. RS, P, N

SOMMELIER WINERY
2560 Wyandotte, Section C, Mountain View 94043
415-969-2442

Tasting by appointment, Saturday, Sunday. Tours by appointment. Picnicking at nearby Mountain View City Park. RS

SYCAMORE CREEK VINEYARDS
12775 Uvas Road, Morgan Hill 95037
408-779-4738
From Highway 101 at Morgan Hill, 3.9 miles on Watsonville Road

Tasting, Saturday, Sunday 12–5. Informal tours and retail sales. Plenty of picnic space as winery is located between two parks. RS

THOMAS KRUSE WINERY
4390 Hecker Pass Road, Gilroy 95020
408-842-7016
From Highway 101 at Morgan Hill, Watsonville Road to Hecker Pass Highway

Tasting daily 12–6. Tours by appointment only. Produces "Chutzpah" wine from Thompson seedless grapes. RS, P

TURGEON & LOHR WINERY
1000 Lenzen Avenue, San Jose 95126
408-288-5057
Off the Alameda, ¼ mile south of Highway 17. 3 miles to airport

Tasting daily 10–5. Tour once each day, Thursday–Sunday. Picnic tables in tasting room. Lunches may be brought in, or special luncheons may be arranged for groups of 10 or more upon advance request. Winery is wheelchair accessible. RS, P

WALKER WINES
25935 Estacada Drive, Los Altos Hills 94022
415-948-6368

Tasting by appointment only. First release of wines is anticipated in fall of 1981.

## Santa Cruz County
Region C

AHLGREN VINEYARD
Box 931, Boulder Creek 95006
408-338-6071
Call or write for appointment and directions.

BARGETTO'S SANTA CRUZ WINERY
3535 North Main Street, Soquel 95073
408-475-2258
4 miles south of Santa Cruz, Capitola-Soquel offramp from Highway 1

Tasting, retail sales, gift shop daily 10–5:30, except major holidays. Tasting room in Monterey at Prescott and Cannery Row. RS, G, J

DAVID BRUCE WINERY
21439 Bear Creek Road, Los Gatos 95030
408-354-4214
5 miles west of Highway 17

Tasting and tours, by appointment only, Saturday 11-2. RS, P, N

DEVLIN WINE CELLARS
North Park Avenue, Soquel 95073
408-476-7288

Tasting and tours Sunday, 12–4, or by appointment. Call winery for directions. RS, P, N

FELTON-EMPIRE VINEYARDS
379 Felton Empire Road, Felton 95018
408-335-3939
2 miles from Highway 9

Tasting and tours Sunday 10–2. State and national parks nearby. RS, P

FRICK WINERY
303 Potrero Street, #39, Santa Cruz 95060
408-426-8623

Call regarding tours and tastings. Usually conducted Friday 11–4. RS, N

GROVER GULCH WINERY
7880 Glen Haven Road, Soquel 95073
408-475-0568

Tasting, retail sales, and tours to begin in 1981, by appointment. First vintage wines, all California reds, will be available at that time. P

NICASIO VINEYARDS
14300 Nicasio Way, Soquel 95073
408-423-1073 or 423-1578

No further information supplied.

RIVER RUN VINTNERS
65 Rogge Lane, Watsonville 95076
408-722-7520
From 101, west on Riverside Drive, Highway 128, 6 miles left on Rogge Lane

Tasting, informal tours, and retail sales by appointment only. Winery is located in apple orchard. Visitors may walk to Pajaro River and have lunch on the beach. Good birdwatching, wading in river. Fresh fruit available at winery's produce stand. Visitors may sign up to help crush grapes. RS, P, J, N

ROUDON-SMITH VINEYARDS
2364 Beaver Road, Santa Cruz 95066
408-438-1244
6 miles north of Santa Cruz, off Mountain View Road

Tasting Saturday 12–4. Tours by appointment. Big Basin Park is nearby. RS

SANTA CRUZ MOUNTAIN VINEYARD
2300 Jarvis Road, Santa Cruz 95065
408-426-6209
8 miles north of Santa Cruz

Tasting by appointment only.

SILVER MOUNTAIN VINEYARDS
P.O. Box 1956, Los Gatos 95030
408-353-2278

Tasting by appointment only.

P AND M STAIGER
1300 Hopkins Gulch Road, Boulder Creek 95006
408-338-4346

No tasting or tours.

SUNRISE WINERY
16001 Empire Grade, Santa Cruz 95060
408-423-8226 or 286-1418

Tours and retail sales. Tasting by appointment. Henry Cowell State Park and Big Basin State Park nearby. RS, P

# Amador County
## Region D

ARGONAUT WINERY
Route 1, Box 612, Ione 95646
209-274-2882 or 274-4106
5 miles northeast of Ione on Willow Creek Road
Tasting and tours by appointment only. RS

D'AGOSTINI WINERY
Route 2, Box 19, Plymouth 95669
209-245-6612
8 miles northeast of Plymouth on Shenandoah Road
Tasting daily 9–4:30. Large groups call for appointment. Winery is a State Historical Landmark. RS

KENWORTHY VINEYARDS
Route 2, Box 2, Plymouth 95669
209-245-3198
East side of Shenandoah Road, ½ mile north of junction of Shenandoah and Fiddletown Roads
Barrel tasting by prior appointment only. Prearranged tours for small groups. RS

MONTEVINA WINES
Route 2, Box 30-A, Plymouth 95669
209-245-3412
3 miles northeast of Plymouth on Shenandoah School Road
Tours by appointment only.

SANTINO WINERY
Route 2, 21A Steiner Road, Plymouth 95669
209-245-3555
Tasting by appointment only. P

SHENANDOAH VINEYARDS
Box 23, Steiner Road, Plymouth 95669
209-245-3698
Shenandoah Road to Steiner Road, follow the vineyards to winery on hill
Tasting and tours by appointment only. RS

STONERIDGE
Route 1, Box 36B, Ridge Road East, Sutter Creek 95685
209-223-1761
2.2 miles east of junction Highway 49 and Ridge Road
Tasting Saturday 1–4, or by appointment. Tours by appointment. RS

# Calaveras County
## Region D

CHISPA CELLARS
425 Main Street, Murphys 95247
209-728-2424 or 728-2106
Tasting and tours by appointment only.

STEVENOT VINEYARDS
Box 548, Murphys 95247
209-728-3893
3 miles north of Murphys on San Domingo Road
Tasting and tours by appointment only. RS, P, J, N

# El Dorado County
## Region D

BOEGER WINERY
1709 Carson Road, Placerville 95667
916-622-8094

Tasting Wednesday–Sunday 10–5. Self-guided tours. Farm-ripened fruit for sale in season. Community college art show in May. RS, P, J

EL DORADO VINEYARDS
3551 Carson Road, Camino 95709
916-644-3773
Highway 50 at Camino turnoff 4 miles east of Placerville

Tasting and tours by appointment.

SIERRA VISTA WINERY
4560 Cabernet Way, Placerville 95667
916-622-7221
At end of Leisure Lane off Pleasant Valley Road

Tasting and tours by appointment only. Picnic tables will be ready by summer 1980, with view of entire Crystal Range of the Sierra. RS, P

## Fresno County
Region D

B. CRIBARI & SONS WINERY
3223 East Church Avenue, Fresno 93727
209-255-0451
From Highway 99 at Jensen Avenue exit east to first signal, left to Church Avenue, turn right.

Tasting daily 10–5. Large groups welcome. RS, J

VILLA BIANCHI WINERY
5806 Modoc Avenue, Kerman 93630
209-846-7356
Tasting Monday–Friday 8–4. A second tasting room is main-

tained at the Queen Mary, Long Beach, open every day 10–7, with museum. RS, J

## Kern County
Region D

GIUMARRA VINEYARDS
P.O. Bin 1969, Bakersfield 93303
805-366-5511
Off Highway 99 in Bakersfield, Highway 58 east 8 miles to Edison Road, left over freeway

Tasting Wednesday–Sunday 9–5. Tours by appointment only. RS, J, N

LAMONT WINERY, INC.
1 Bear Mountain Winery Road, DiGiorgio 93217
805-327-2200
10 miles east of Highway 99, 5 miles south of Highway 58 near DiGiorgio Road and Comanche Road

Tasting and tours Tuesday–Saturday 10–5. RS, G, J

A. PERELLI-MINETTI & SONS WINERY
P.O. Box 818, Delano 93216
805-792-3162
Adjacent to freeway at Pond Road and Highway 99. 3 miles south of Delano, 28 miles north of Bakersfield

Tasting and tours daily 10–5. RS, P

## Madera County
Region D

ANGELO PAPAGNI VINEYARDS
31754 Avenue 9, Madera 93637
209-674-5652
6 miles south on Highway 99 and Avenue 0

No tasting. Tours by appointment only. RS, N

COARSEGOLD WINE CELLAR
Route 2, Coarsegold 93614
209-683-4850
On Highway 41, 3 miles south of Coarsegold

Tasting daily 10–5.

FICKLIN VINEYARDS
30246 Avenue 7½, Madera 93637
209-674-4598

No tasting or tours. Small family winery only producing Ficklin Tinta Port at this time.

QUADY WINERY
13181 Road 24, Madera 93637
209-674-8696

Tasting and tours by appointment only. Produces only vintage Port. RS

## Sacramento County
Region D

GIBSON WINE CO.
9750 Kent, Elk Grove 95624
916-685-9594
Highway 99 at Grant Line Road, 3 miles south of Elk Grove

Tasting and retail sales at Highway 99 and Grant Line Road, not at winery, daily 10–6. Produces fruit and berry wines. RS, G, P, J

JAMES FRASINETTI & SONS
P.O. Box 28213, Sacramento 95812
916-383-2444
Highway 99 to Florin Road, east to Frasinetti Road

Tasting Monday–Saturday 9–6, Sunday 11–6. RS

## San Joaquin County
Region D

BARENGO VINEYARDS
3125 East Orange Street, Acampo 95220
209-369-2746
1 mile west of Highway 99

Tasting, sales, and gift shop 9–5 (winter); 9–6 (summer). Local Lodi Art Show, third weekend in May. Winery also has tasting rooms in Dixon off I-80, just east of Nut Tree Restaurant; Red Bluff on I-5; Farmers Markets, Los Angeles and Santa Fe Springs, Southern California. RS, G, P, J

CALIFORNIA CELLAR MASTERS
P.O. Box 478, Lodi 95240
209-368-7822
North Highway 99 frontage road

Tasting, sales, and gifts Tuesday–Sunday 10–5. Also at The Old Winery Complex, Escalon; The Way Station, Cayucos (San Luis Obispo County); Columbia State Park and Old Town Sacramento, 130 K Street. RS, G

DELICATO VINEYARDS
12001 South Highway 99, Manteca 95336
209-239-1215 or 982-0679
From Highway 99, 4.2 miles north of Manteca

Tasting daily 9–5. Tours by appointment only. Many public parks nearby for picnicking. RS, G, J, N

EAST-SIDE WINERY
6100 East Highway 12, Lodi 95240
209-369-4768

Tasting and tours daily 9–5. Lodi Grape Festival and National Wine Show (September 18–21, 1980.) RS, P, J

FRANZIA BROS. WINERY
P.O. Box 697, Ripon 95366
209-599-4111
6 miles east of Manteca on Yosemite Avenue (Highway 120)

Tasting daily 10–5. RS, P

GUILD'S CENTRAL CELLARS
1 Winemasters Way, Lodi 95240
209-368-5151
½ mile east of Highway 99 on Highway 12, left on Myrtle Avenue

Tasting and tours daily 10–5. Catered luncheons and dinner by prearrangement. Summer concert series. Display vineyard. RS, P

LIBERTY WINERY
6055 East Acampo Road, Acampo 95220
209-368-6646

Producer of bulk wines only. Tours for groups of six or under may be arranged by calling.

LUCAS HOME WINE
18196 North Davis, Lodi 95240
209-368-2006
Highway 99 west on Turner

Tasting and retail sales October–December 20 only. Tours by appointment. Sells by mailing list. Produces only Zinfandel. RS, P

TURNER WINERY
3750 East Woodbridge Road, Acampo 95220
209-368-5338
Tasting will begin in fall of 1980.

## Stanislaus County
Region D

E. & J. GALLO WINERY
600 Yosemite Boulevard, Modesto 95353
209-521-3111
No tasting or tours.

PIRRONE WINE CELLARS
P.O. Box 15, Salida 95368
209-545-0704
From Highway 99, 6.5 miles north of Modesto on Pirrone Road
Tasting Monday–Friday 9–5.

## Tulare County
Region D

CALIFORNIA GROWERS WINERY, INC.
P.O. Box 21, Yettem, 93670
209-528-3033
Approximately ½ mile west of Yettem, east on Avenue 384 from Highway 99
Tasting Monday–Friday 1–4. Tours by appointment only.

## Tuolumne County
Region D

YANKEE HILL WINERY
P.O. Box 163, Columbia 95310
209-532-3015
¾ mile east of Columbia, Yankee Hill Road
Tasting and tours sunup to sundown. RS, P

# Yolo County
## Region D

R AND J COOK WINERY
Netherlands Road, Clarksburg
95612
916-775-1234

Not open to the public until late
1980.

HARBOR WINERY
610 Harbor Boulevard, West Sacramento 95831
916-371-6776 or 392-7954

Not open to the public.

# Los Angeles County
## Region E

AHERN WINERY
715 Arroyo Avenue, San Fernando
91340
213-361-0349

Tours Saturday, Sunday by appointment only.

THE MARTIN WINERY
11800 West Jefferson Boulevard,
Culver City 90230
213-390-5736

Tasting Monday–Thursday 11–7;
Friday, Saturday 11–8; Sunday
11–6.

Wines from other areas may be
sampled as well as the Martin
Winery wines. RS

SAN ANTONIO WINERY
737 Lamar Street, Los Angeles
90031
213-223-1401

Tasting Monday–Saturday 9–8,
Sunday 10–6. RS, G, P

# Riverside County
## Region E

CALLAWAY VINEYARD AND WINERY
32720 Rancho California Road,
Temecula 92390
714-676-4001

31 miles south of Riverside on
Highway 15E, take offramp,
Rancho California Road, east
approximately 4 miles

Tasting for professionals in industry only. Tours, hourly, 11–4.
Outdoor barbecue and tables for
private parties by special arrangement. Charge of $15.00
per person. RS, P

CILURZO & PICONI WINERY
41220 Calle Contento, Temecula
92390
714-676-5250

Between San Diego and Riverside
on Highway 15, exit at Rancho
California Road, east 6 miles,
right on Calle Contento ¼ mile

No tasting. Tours by appointment.
Picnic area in preparation. RS

GALLEANO WINERY, INC.
4231 Wineville Road, Mira Loma
91752
714-685-5376

1 mile east of Milliken, ½ mile
south on Wineville Road

Tasting Monday–Saturday 8–6.
Tours by appointment only.
Jurupa Cultural Center nearby.
Picnic area under development.
RS, G, J

GLENOAK HILLS WINERY
Box 883, Temecula 93290
714-676-5831

No tasting or tours. Call winery for appointment or directions.

MOUNT PALOMAR WINERY
33820 Rancho California Road, Temecula 92390
714-676-5047
From Highway 15, exit Rancho California Road, 6 miles east

Tasting daily, except Christmas, New Year's, and Thanksgiving, 9–5. Tours 11:30, 1:30, 3:30. Deli items. Visitors welcome to walk vineyard roads. RS, G, P, J

OPICI WINERY, INC.
P.O. Box 56, Alta Loma 91701
714-987-2710
5 miles from Highway 10 on Haven Avenue offramp, north to Highland

Tasting daily 10-6.

PRESTIGE VINEYARDS AND HADLEY'S FRUIT ORCHARDS
48980 Seminole Drive, Cabazon 92230
714-849-4668

Tasting and retail sales 8–7:30 daily. No tours. RS

## San Bernardino County
Region E

BROOKSIDE WINERY
9900 Guasti Road, Guasti 91743
714-983-2787
Guasti Road at Archibald Avenue off San Bernardino freeway

Tasting daily 8–7. RS, P

J. FILIPPI VINTAGE CO.
P.O. Box 2, Mira Loma 91752
714-984-4514

1¼ miles south of San Bernardino freeway on Etiwanda Avenue

Tasting daily 10–6. RS, P

LOUIS CHERPIN WINERY
15567 Valley Boulevard, Fontana 92335
714-822-4103
Highway 10 between Cherry and Citrus

Tasting daily 8–5. RS

THOMAS VINEYARDS
8916 Foothill Boulevard, Cucamonga 91730
714-987-1612
½ mile west of Cucamonga on Foothill Boulevard and Vineyard Avenue. Four miles north of Ontario airport

Tasting and self-conducted tours daily 8–6. Gift shop inside large wine tank. Antique winery equipment display. Winery is a State Historical Landmark. Expect to open restaurant on premises soon. Tables and barbecue on patio. RS, G, P, J

## San Diego County
Region E

BERNARDO WINERY
13330 Paseo Del Verano Norte, San Diego 92128
714-487-1866
Pomerado Road off Route 15 (Highway 66) 7 miles south of Escondido

Tasting daily 7–6. Antiques, silversmith, and art studio. Deli. RS, P

FERRARA WINERY
1120 West 15th Avenue, Escondido 92025
714-745-7632
West on Felicita Avenue from Centre City Parkway, right on Redwood Avenue to 15th Avenue

Tasting and self-conducted tours daily 9–6:30. RS

SAN PASQUAL VINEYARDS
13455 San Pasqual Road, Escondido 92025
714-741-0855
3 miles south of Escondido on Highway 395, take Via Rancho Parkway off, east 1 mile to San Pasqual Road

Tasting at Saturday open house 10–4. Tours by appointment. Three miles from San Diego Wild Animal Park. Picnic area in preparation. J

# Wine
# Publications

# Introduction

Probably one of the first things a winery decides to do, after the harvest and the first crush, is tell the world about its uniqueness — the wine, the place, and people who produced it. The easiest way, sitting around in the cold winter months, is to write a newsletter, but sustaining that report to the people can become quite another thing, particularly as the year wears on, and another harvest and crush is on the way. Many wineries do, however, produce newsletters on a monthly, bi-monthly, quarterly, or now-and-then basis. They serve to announce new releases or improvements at the winery and often include some personal notes from the winemaker. The best have been around for several decades, and they are an unending source of information for the wine buff. Many take the reader through the seasons in the life of a grape, with illustrations and critical observations. Almost all of them are free, and most will add your name to the mailing list within four to six weeks after receiving your request. If you request sample copies, be sure to enclose $1.00 for postage and handling.

In addition to newsletters and bulletins produced by the wineries, an ever-growing number of wine writers offer letters of their own that include commentary, wine evaluations, tasting notes, and profiles of wineries from coast to coast. A poll of these writers has resulted in the list you will find in the following pages. Those produced outside the state of California frequently deal with the wines of this state. For wine lovers anywhere in the nation, these letters provide valuable information about California wines that have traveled to various locales and where California wines can be purchased locally.

More ambitious are the wine magazines, assembled and issued at varying times. Some are an added benefit that accompanies membership in one of the wine associations or societies with chapters throughout the nation or internationally. One or two started out to be highly technical publications, but they discovered their audience wanted more general news and so expanded.

At the end of this section, you will find a selection of books either written exclusively about California wines, or containing excellent California sections and/or references. But there are new wine books coming out every day, as you will see on a visit to your local bookstore. For the serious collector, a few catalog sources round out this report.

# Newsletters-
# Winery

## Napa County
### Region A

BERINGER VINEYARDS
2000 Main Street
St. Helena 94574

*Beringer Vineyard Report* (quarterly). Technical, soil types, acid and sugar information, viticultural aspects of wine growing, harvests, new releases of particular interest.

CAKEBREAD CELLARS
P.O. Box 216
Rutherford 94573

*Untitled* (as new wines are released). Listing of new releases, how the wines were made, news of the winery.

CASSAYRE-FORNI CELLARS
1271 Manley Lane
Rutherford 94573

*Untitled* (no set schedule). Lists new releases, general winery information, description of wine, particulars of chemical components, prices.

CHARLES KRUG WINERY
P.O. Box 191
St. Helena 94574

*Bottles and Bins* (quarterly). Temporarily suspended. Will resume. Wine editorials, listings of good books, recipe column.

CHATEAU MONTELENA
1429 Tubbs Lane
Calistoga 94515

*News from the Chateau* (monthly). General information of happenings at the winery, news about wines and special items available at winery.

HANNS KORNELL CHAMPAGNE CELLARS ✓
P.O. Box 249
St. Helena 94574

*Champagne News* (seasonal, 4 times a year). General information regarding champagne making, storing, etc.; recipe section.

INGLENOOK VINEYARDS
P.O. Box 19
Rutherford 94573

*Inglenook News* (quarterly). Wide range of information: harvest report, aging charts, interview with the winemaker, new releases.

MAYACAMAS VINEYARDS
1155 Lokoya Road
Napa 94558

No further information supplied.

RODDIS CELLAR
1510 Diamond Mountain Road
Calistoga 94515

No further information supplied.

STERLING VINEYARDS
P.O. Box 365
Calistoga 94515

*A Letter to the Friends of Sterling* (three or four times a year). New wine releases, overall impression of the year, what is happening at the winery.

STONEGATE WINERY
1183 Dunaweal Lane
Calistoga 94515

*Untitled* (twice a year, spring and fall). New releases, production, prices, expansion, news of the winery.

## Humboldt County
Region B

FIELDBROOK VALLEY WINERY
Route 1, Box 314
Fieldbrook 95521

No further information supplied.

## Mendocino County
Region B

MILANO WINERY
14594 South Highway 101
Hopland 95449

*Newsletter* (once or twice a year). Information on new releases, harvest, winery additions.

## Sonoma County
Region B

ALEXANDER VALLEY VINEYARDS
8644 Highway 128
Healdsburg 95448

*Untitled* (twice a year). New releases with a description of the wines.

BUENA VISTA WINERY, INC.
P.O. Box 182
Sonoma 95476

*Buena Vista News* (seasonally). General viticultural information, technical details.

CHATEAU ST. JEAN
P.O. Box 293
Kenwood 95452

No further information supplied.

GEYSER PEAK WINERY
P.O. Box 25
Geyserville 95441

*News from the Peak* (irregularly). General information about winery and wines.

GRAND CRU VINEYARDS
P.O. Drawer B
Glen Ellen 95442

In planning stages.

HACIENDA WINE CELLARS
P.O. Box 416
Sonoma 95476

*Hacienda Wine Press* (seasonally). Harvest and general information, new releases, questions and answers, recipes.

HOP KILN WINERY
6050 Westside Road
Healdsburg 95448

*Untitled* (quarterly). New releases, general wine information, awards won, order form for ordering wines.

JOHNSON'S ALEXANDER VALLEY WINERY
8333 Highway 128
Healdsburg 95448

*Johnson's Newsletter* (three times a year). New product information, events at the winery.

LYTTON SPRINGS WINERY, INC.
650 Lytton Springs Road
Healdsburg 95448

*Untitled* (when new wines are released). New release information, order form.

NERVO WINERY
P.O. Box 25
Geyserville 95441

*Friends of Nervo* (prior to major holidays). Information about up-coming sales, recipes.

SEBASTIANI VINEYARDS
P.O. Box AA
Sonoma 95476

*Sebastiani Vineyards* (monthly). General information about wines, growing, processing.

SIMI WINERY
P.O. Box 946
Healdsburg 95448

*Simi News* (irregularly). General information about winery and wines.

SONOMA VINEYARDS
P.O. Box 368
Windsor 95492

No further information supplied.

SOUVERAIN CELLARS
P.O. Box 528
Geyserville 95441

*Souverain Limited Edition* (seasonally). Announcements of happenings at the winery, awards won, wine prognostications.

## Alameda County
Region C

CONCANNON VINEYARDS
P.O. Box 432
Livermore 94550

*Vineyard Vignettes* (twice a year). General information, recipes, personality profiles, new releases.

MONTCLAIR WINERY
180 Maxwelton Road
Piedmont 94618
No further information supplied.

NUMANO SAKE COMPANY
708 Addison Street
Berkeley 94710
*Numano's Newsletter*

WENTE BROS. WINERY
5565 Tesla Road
Livermore 94550
*Newsletter* (no set schedule). General information about winery and personnel.

## Monterey County
Region C

MONTEREY PENINSULA WINERY
2999 Monterey-Salinas Highway
Monterey 93940
*Newsletter* (annual, fall). General winery information.

THE MONTEREY VINEYARD
P.O. Box 780
Gonzales 93926
*Winemaker Notes* (monthly or bi-monthly). General information on wine, winemaking, and Monterey County growing conditions.

VENTANA VINEYARDS WINERY
P.O. Box G, Los Coches Road
Soledad 93960

*Untitled* (twice a year). Information on new releases, history of the county, winery news.

## San Luis Obispo County
Region C

HOFFMAN MOUNTAIN RANCH VINEYARDS
Adelaida Road, Star Route
Paso Robles 93446
*HMR Newsletter* (quarterly). Current events, technical data, acids and sugars, new releases.

## Santa Barbara County
Region C

ZACA MESA WINERY
Foxen Canyon Road
Los Olivos 93441
Still in planning stages.

## Santa Clara County
Region C

CONGRESS SPRINGS VINEYARDS
23600 Congress Springs Road
Saratoga 95070
*Untitled* (annually). Announcement of public tasting, which wines will be tasted, other new releases, map of route to winery.

GEMELLO WINERY, INC.
2003 El Camino Real
Mountain View 94040
*Gemello Newsletter* (annually). Social information, new releases, includes news of releases of other wineries in area.

KIRIGIN CELLARS
11550 Watsonville Road
Gilroy 95020

*Kirigin Cellars* (occasionally). New releases of wines, social events, additions to winery.

MIRASSOU VINEYARDS
3000 Aborn Road
San Jose 95135

*Latest Press* (three times a year). Winery events, wines, harvest, new releases, recipes, aging charts.

PAUL MASSON VINEYARDS
13150 Saratoga Avenue
Saratoga 95070

*Grapeline* (no set schedule.) General winery information, new releases, special events.

SAN MARTIN WINERY
P.O. Box 53
San Martin 95046

*San Martin Winery Newsletter* (seasonal, four times a year). A cover story with pictures, new wine releases, recipes with pictures, winemaster notes, focus story on winery feature.

SHERRILL CELLARS
P.O. Box 4155
Woodside 94062

*Untitled* (four times a year). New releases, winery happenings, descriptions of educational wine tastings held at winery.

## Santa Cruz County
## Region C

DAVID BRUCE WINERY
21439 Bear Creek Road
Los Gatos 95030

*Untitled* (twice a year). New releases, winery events, winemaker notes.

DEVLIN WINE CELLARS
P.O. Box 723
Soquel 95073

*Untitled* (every 6 months). New releases, winemaking notes.

FRICK WINERY
303 Potrero Street, #39
Santa Cruz 95060

*New Wine Releases* (two or three times a year). Descriptions of wine, winemaker notes, general information.

RIVER RUN VINTNERS
65 Rogge Lane
Watsonville, 95076

*River Run Vintners Wine Press* (quarterly). New wine releases, what's happening in the area.

## Calaveras County
## Region D

STEVENOT WINERY
P.O. Box 548
Murphys 95247

No further information supplied.

# Kern County
## Region D

GIUMARRA VINEYARDS
P.O. Bin 1969
Bakersfield 93303

*Giumarra Family Grapevine* (seasonal, four times a year). Winery features with technical details about wine, notes from winemaker, "John on Wine."

A. PERELLI-MINETTI & SONS WINERY
P.O. Box 818
Delano 93216

*California Wine Advisor* (six times a year). General information about winemaking, wine regulations, recipes, winemaker notes. (By subscription: $3.00 per year).

# Madera County
## Region D

ANGELO PAPAGNI VINEYARDS
31754 Avenue 9
Madera 93637

*Papagni Press* (three or four times a year). General winery information.

# San Joaquin County
## Region D

DELICATO VINEYARDS
12001 South Highway 99
Manteca 95336

*Meet Delicato* (monthly). General information about tastings, glasses, new releases, recipes.

# Newsletters – Privately Produced (Subscription)

## California

ROBERT BALZER'S PRIVATE GUIDE TO FOOD AND WINE
12791 Newport Avenue, Tustin 92680

Author: Robert Balzer; eleven times a year; $22.50 per year.

BOTTLES UP
470 Columbus Avenue, San Francisco 94133

Author: Fred Cherry; monthly; $25.00 per year.

CALIFORNIA GRAPEVINE
P.O. Box 22152, San Diego 92122

Author: Nicholas A. Ponomareff; bi-monthly; $15.00 per year.

CALIFORNIA WINELETTER
P.O. Box 70, Mill Valley 94941

Author: Phyllis van Kriedt; semi-monthly; $35.00 per year.

CONNOISSEURS' GUIDE TO CALIFORNIA WINE
P.O. Box 11120, San Francisco 94101

Authors: Earl Singer, Charles Olken; bi-monthly; $20.00 per year.

THE CRUSH
926 J Street, Suite 416, Sacramento 95814

Published by California Association of Wine Grape Growers exclusively for its members.

ROBERT FINIGAN'S PRIVATE GUIDE TO WINES
100 Bush Street, San Francisco 94104
Author: Robert Finigan; monthly; $24.00 per year.

NOTES FOR THE FRUGAL ENOPHILE
P.O. Box 6861, Burbank 91510
Author: J. D. Kronman; ten times a year; $15.00 per year.

UNDERGROUND WINELETTER
P.O. Box 663, Seal Beach 90740
Author: John Tilson; bi-monthly; $20.00 per year.

WHITTIER WINE SOCIETY NEWSLETTER
6230 Hill Avenue, Whittier 90601
Author: Marylee von Otteman; quarterly; $15.00 per year, with membership in Whittier Wine Society.

W.I.N.O.
13910 La Jolla Plaza, Garden Grove 92640
Author: Jerry Mead; six times a year, minimum; $15.00 per year, included with membership in organization.

WINE ALERT
P.O. Box 805, Larkspur 94939
Author: Michael Hildebrand; twenty-two times a year; $125.00 per year.

WINE BUFF
Esplanade III, Suite 216, 3001 Red Hill Avenue, Costa Mesa 92626
Author: Fred Russell; monthly; $18.00 per year.

WINE DISCOVERIES
P.O. Box 654, El Cerrito 94530
Author: Arthur Damond; bi-monthly; $8.50 per year.

WINE INVESTOR
6430 Sunset Boulevard, Los Angeles 90028
Author: Paul Gillette; semi-monthly; $100.00 per year (executive edition), $30.00 buyer's guide.

WINE NEWSLETTER
P.O. Box 255214, Sacramento 95825
Author: Dr. Frank Herand; six times a year; no charge.

THE WINE SCENE
10982 Roebling Avenue, #532, Los Angeles 90024
Author: John D. Movius; six times a year; $9.00 per year.

THE WINE TRADE
716 Wisconsin Street, San Francisco 94107
Authors: Ed and Anna Everett; monthly; $40.00 per year; overseas $50.00 per year.

## Outside California
### Colorado

ROCKY MOUNTAIN WINE GUIDE
P.O. Box 203, Englewood, CO 80110
Author: Bob Slakowitz; bi-monthly; $9.00 per year.

## Connecticut

WINE LINES
P.O. Box 1274, Middletown, CT 06457
Author: Anthony F. Price; monthly; $15.00 per year.

## Florida

WINE LETTER
975 Marigold Lane, Vero Beach, FL 32960
Author: Ernest G. Sloan; monthly; $18.00 per year.

## Hawaii

WINE SOCIETY NEWSLETTER
361-C Hualani Street, Kailua, HI 96734
Author: Harry C. Fernald; monthly; $12.00 per year.

## Illinois

ARNOLD LANDSMAN'S WINE LETTER
188 West Randolph Street, Chicago, IL 60610
Author: Arnold Landsman; six times a year; $20.00 per year.

## Minnesota

BACCHUS NEWSLETTER
23 South 7th Street, Minneapolis, MN 55402
Author: John Farrell; monthly; distributed through member retail shops.

## New Jersey

THE WINE NEWSLETTER
Box 279, Franklin Lakes, NJ 07417
Authors: Sheldon and Pauline Wasserman; monthly; $25.00 per year.

## New Mexico

BON VIVANT WINE GUIDE
Box 25401, Albuquerque, NM 87125
Author: Stephen Farrelly; monthly; $9.85 per year.

## New York

CASES NEWSLETTER
230 West 79th Street, New York, NY 10024
Author: Ronald A. Kapon; monthly; $24.00 per year.

CONSUMER WINELETTER
Box 135, Irvington, NY 10533
Author: Henri Fluchere; monthly; $20.00

IMPACT
305 East 53rd Street, New York, NY 10022
Author: Marvin Shanken; semi-monthly; $72.00 per year.

THE WINE & DINE NEWSLETTER
60 Sheridan Ave., Williston Park, NY 11596
Author: Robert Lipinski; monthly; $12.00 per year.

## Pennsylvania

PENNSYLVANIA GRAPE LETTER &
WINE NEWS
620 N. Pine Street, Lancaster, PA
17603
Author: Hudson Cattell; ten times
a year; $6.50 per year.

## Texas

THE GRAPE GROUP
P.O. Box 189, Dallas, TX 75231
Author: Various; distributed by
member retail shops.

MOODY'S WINE REVIEW
1307 Post Oak Park Drive, Houston, TX 77027
Author: Denman Moody, Jr.; quarterly; $20.00 per year.

## Utah

WINELETTER
1048 Oak Hills Way, Salt Lake
City, UT 84108
Author: Col. Jack E. Daniels;
quarterly; free to members.

## Washington

NORTHWEST CONSUMERS WINE GUIDE
P.O. Box 15380, Seattle, WA
98115
Author: Eugene Stein; monthly;
$15.00 per year.

# Periodicals

AMERICAN WINE JOURNAL
4218 Rosewold Avenue, Royal Oak, MI 48073

Published by American Wine Society; quarterly; included in annual dues, $12.50 per year.

THE ARBOR
P.O. Box 13285, Sacramento, CA 95813

Published by Brotherhood of the Knights of the Vine; included in annual dues or $10.00 per year to nonmembers.

THE FRIENDS OF WINE
2302 Perkins Place, Silver Springs, MD 20910

Published by Les Amis du Vin; bi-monthly; included in annual dues or $12.00 per year to nonmembers.

GRAPPA
P.O. Box 221127, Carmel, CA 93922

Published six times a year; $35.00 per year.

VINTAGE
P.O. Box 11779, Philadelphia, PA 19101

Published by The Vintage Society; monthly; included in annual dues of $25.00.

THE WINE SPECTATOR
4017 Brant Street, San Diego, CA 92103

Editor: Bob Morrisey; semimonthly; $25.00 per year.

WINES & VINES
703 Market Street, San Francisco, CA 94103
Editor: Phil Hiaring; monthly; $16.00 per year.

WINE WORLD
15101 Keswick Street, Van Nuys, CA 91405
Editor: Dee Sindt; bi-monthly; $14.00 per year.

# Selected Books

Abel, Dominick. 1979.   *Guide to the Wines of the United States.* New York: Cornerstone.

Adams, Leon D. 1975.   *The Commonsense Book of Wine.* Boston: Houghton Mifflin, with San Francisco Book Co. Revised and Expanded.

Adams, Leon D. 1978.   *The Wines of America.* New York: McGraw-Hill. 2nd Edition Revised.

Amerine, Maynard A., and Singleton, Vernon L. 1977.   *Wine: An Introduction.* Berkeley: University of California Press. 2nd Edition.

Balzer, Robert L. 1973.   *Robert Lawrence Balzer's Book of Wines and Spirits.* Los Angeles: Ward Ritchie.

Balzer, Robert L. 1978.   *Wines of California.* New York: Abrams.

Benson, Robert. 1977.   *Great Winemakers of California.* Santa Barbara, California: Capra Press.

Bespaloff, Alexis. 1980.   *The New Signet Book of Wine: A Complete Introduction.* New York: New American Library.

Chroman, Nathan. 1973. *The Treasury of American Wines*. New York: Rutledge-Crown.

Fisher, M.F.K. 1962. *The Story of Wine in California*. Photographs by Max Yavno. Berkeley: University of California Press.

Gillette, Paul. 1976. *Enjoying Wine*. New York: New American Library/Signet.

Greenberg, Emanuel and Madeline. 1977. *Great Cooks' Guide to Wine Drinks*. New York: Beard Glaser Wolf.

Hazelton, Nika. 1976. *American Wines*. New York: Grosset & Dunlap.

Henriques, E. Frank. 1975. *The Signet Encyclopedia of Wine*. New York: New American Library/Signet.

Hinkle, Richard Paul. 1977. *Central Coast Wine Tour*. St. Helena, California: Vintage Image.

Hinkle, Richard Paul. 1979 *Napa Valley Wine Book*. St. Helena, California: Vintage Image.

Johnson, Hugh. 1979. *Pocket Encyclopedia of Wine*. New York: Simon & Schuster.

Mackenzie, Alexander. 1978. *California's Top Ten Wines*. Los Angeles: Armstrong Publishing.

Melville, John. 1976. *Guide to California Wines*. New York: Dutton. 5th Edition, Revised by Jefferson Morgan.

Quimme, Peter. 1980. *The Signet Book of American Wine*. New York: New American Library/Signet. 3rd Edition.

Ramey, Bern. 1977. *The Great Wine Grapes and the Wines They Make*. Burlingame, California: Great Wine Grapes, Inc.

Schoenman, Theodore. 1979. *The Father of California Wine: Agoston Haraszthy*. Santa Barbara, California: Capra Press.

Seward, Desmond. 1979. *Monks and Wine*. New York: Crown Press.

Sunset Books. 1979. *Guide to California's Wine Country*. Menlo Park, California: Lane Publishing. Research: Robert Thompson. Consultant: Margaret Smith.

Thompson, Robert. 1976. *The California Wine Book*. New York: Morrow.

## Catalogs

Les Amis du Vin
Wine and Food Library
2302 Perkins Place
Silver Springs, MD 20910

Free to members

Wholesale Book List
The Wine Appreciation Guild
1377 Ninth Avenue
San Francisco, CA 94122

No charge

Catalog 979
Elisabeth Woodburn
Booknoll Farm
Hopewell, NJ 08525

$1.50

The Wine and Food Library
1207 W. Madison
Ann Arbor, MI 48103

$2.00

NOTE: The Wine Institute, which represents the wineries of California, offers a free correspondence course on California wine. Write: Wine Study Course, Wine Institute, 165 Post St., San Francisco, CA 94108.

# Restaurants
# and Retail Stores

# Introduction

Short of traveling across the nation and dining at every available restaurant or shopping for California wines at every available retail wine shop, there does not seem to be any practical way of gathering information about wine lists and wine sales. So without time or resources for this kind of tour, we turned to the people most apt to know where California wines are showcased. These people, the leading food and wine writers of the country, by the very nature of their profession eat out a lot and examine with special care the wine lists and menus in dining establishments of all sizes and types. In order to conduct and participate in wine tastings and coordinate foods with wines, they are also most likely to know where to go in each of the major cities to obtain that elusive bottle of Mendocino Riesling, Amador County Zinfandel, or Santa Barbara Cabernet Sauvignon.

The suggestions from the men and women who write the wine news have been assembled and are listed here. Anyone should, and undoubtedly will, try the wines of each state, but when the palate will just not be satisfied with anything less than the perfected contents of a bottle bearing a California label, you can turn to this list and find an old friend.

# Restaurants

## California

A La Carte    2055 N. Broadway, Walnut Creek
Ambrosia    501 30th St., Newport Beach
Andalou    5th & E Streets, San Rafael
Anthony's Pier 2    103 N. Bayside, Newport Beach
Antonello    South Coast Plaza Village, Santa Ana
Bay Wolf    3853 Piedmont Ave., Oakland
Calistoga Inn    1250 Lincoln Ave., Calistoga
Cask 'n Cleaver    various Southern California locations
Chez Cary    571 So. Main, Orange
Chez Panisse    1517 Shattuck Ave., Berkeley
Chronicle    897 Granite Dr., Pasadena
The Cliff House    1090 Point Lobos Ave., San Francisco
Depot Hotel    241 First St. West, Sonoma
Domaine Chandon    California Dr., Yountville
Emile's Swiss Affair    545 South 2nd St., San Jose
English Grill    St. Francis Hotel, Union Square, San Francisco
Ernie's    847 Montgomery St., San Francisco

The Firehouse Wine Bar      414 Calle Principal, Monterey
Fournou's Ovens      Stanford Court, 905 California St., San Francisco
464 Magnolia      464 Magnolia Ave., Larkspur
French Laundry      6640 Washington, Yountville
Imperial Dynasty      China Row, Hanford
Lake Merritt Wine & Cheese Revival      552 Grand Ave., Oakland
La Maison de Pescadoux      2265 Bacon, San Diego
L'Etoile      1075 California St., San Francisco
The London Wine Bar      415 Sansome St., San Francisco
MacArthur Park      607 Front St., San Francisco
Mama Nina's      6772 Washington, Yountville
Michael's      4500 Los Feliz Blvd., Los Angeles
Modesto Lanzone's      900 North Point, San Francisco
Mr. Stox      1105 E. Katella, Anaheim
Narsai's      385 Colusa Ave., Berkeley
North Beach Restaurant      1512 Stockton, San Francisco
The Nut Tree      County Airport Rd., Vacaville
Peppone's      11628 Barrington Ct., Brentwood
Redwood Room      Clift Hotel, Geary & Taylor Streets, San Francisco
Riccardo's      441 San Anselmo Ave., San Anselmo
Rive Gauche      33 West Portal Ave., San Francisco
Saloon      Santa Monica & Canon, Beverly Hills
The Sardine Factory      701 Wave, Monterey
Scandia      9040 Sunset, Los Angeles
Silverado Restaurant      1374 Lincoln, Calistoga
Slocum House      7992 California Ave., Fair Oaks
The Squire Restaurant      Fairmont Hotel, California at Mason,
   San Francisco
Trader Vic's      San Francisco and Los Angeles
Valentino's      3115 Pico Blvd., Santa Monica
Victor's      St. Francis Hotel, Union Square, San Francisco
The Vintner      1875 Union St., San Francisco
Vintner's Pantry      1500 Golden Gateway, Lafayette
Walnut Creek Wine & Cheese Co.      1522 N. Main St., Walnut Creek

# Colorado

Apple Tree Shanty      8710 E. Colfax, Denver
Broiler      821 17th St., Denver
Ichabod's Cafe      7095 E. Evans, Denver

# Connecticut

Fatone Brothers Restaurant     156 West Main St., Niantic
Yankee Silversmith     Rt. 5, Wallingford

# Delaware

The Crab Shack     130 S. DuPont Hwy., New Castle

# Florida

Bern's Steak House     1208 S. Howard Ave., Tampa
Casa Vecchia     209 N. Birch Rd., Ft. Lauderdale
Club 41     432 Arthur Godfrey Rd., Miami Beach
The Down Under     3000 E. Oakland Park Blvd., Ft. Lauderdale
The Forge     432 Arthur Godfrey Rd., Miami Beach
La Vieille Maison (Leaonce Picot)     770 E. Palmett Pk. Rd., Boca Raton
The Menu     1517 S. Ocean Dr., Vero Beach
The Surf Restaurant     Fernadina Beach, Fernadina
The Village South     2900 Ocean Dr., Vero Beach

# Georgia

The Abbey Restaurant     Piedmont and Ponce de Leon, Atlanta
The Midnight Sun     225 Peachtree Center, Atlanta

# Idaho

Annabel's     1302 Vista Ave., Boise
Remo's     160 W. Cedar, Pocatello
Remo's     340 E. Anderson, Idaho Falls

# Illinois

Bastille     21 W. Superior St., Chicago
Chestnut Grill     845 N. Michigan, Chicago
Del Rios     228 Greenbay, Highwood
Eugene's     1255 N. State Pkwy., Chicago
Geja's     340 W. Armitage Ave, Chicago
Gitanes     2350 N. Clark St., Chicago
Jerome's     2450 N. Clark St., Chicago
Paradise Cafe     3352 N. Broadway, Chicago
Village Smithy     368 Park Ave, Glencoe

## Massachusetts

The Bunch of Grapes     Faneuil Hall Market Place, Boston
Pier Four     140 Northern Ave., Boston

## Michigan

Bacchus Tastevin     6216 S. Westnedge Ave., Portage
Beggars Banquet     218 Abbott Rd., East Lansing
London Chop House     155 W. Congress, Detroit
Vargo's     30325 Six Mile Rd., Livonia

## Minnesota

The Lowell Inn     102 No. Second St., Stillwater

## Mississippi

Lyle Bonge's     1433 W. Howard, Biloxi

## Missouri

The Monastery     6227 Brookside, Kansas City
The Souper     431 Westport Rd., Kansas City

## Nebraska

French Cafe     1017 Howard, Omaha
V. Mertz     1022 Howard St., Omaha

## New Hampshire

Country Gourmet     Rt. 3, D.W. Highway, Merrimack

## New Jersey

The Quay     280 Ocean Ave., Sea Bright
Summit House     510 Summit Ave., Jersey City

# New York

E. F. Barrett & Co.     102 E. 22nd St., New York
Caliban     360 Third Ave., New York
Claret's     337 E. 60th St., New York
Coach House     110 Waverly Place, New York
The Four Seasons     99 W. 52nd St., New York
Gage & Tollner     372 Fulton St., Brooklyn
Garvin's Restaurant     19 Waverly Place, New York
L'Auberge du Cochon Rouge     Danby Rd., Ithaca
Le Pont Neuf     212 E. 53rd St., New York
Oyster Bar & Restaurant     Grand Central Station, New York
River Cafe     1 Water St., Brooklyn
6 Plaisir     969 Lexington Ave., New York
Spark's Steakhouse     46th St. & Third Ave., New York
U.S. Steakhouse     120 W. 51st St., New York
Windows on the World     World Trade Center, New York
The Wine Bar     422 W. Broadway, New York
The Wine Bistro, Ltd.     201 E. 64th St., New York
The Wine Press Wine Bar     1160 First Ave., New York

# North Carolina

The Carolina Inn     West Cameron Ave., Chapel Hill

# Oregon

Belinda's     8324 S.E. 17th, Portland
London Grill     Benson Hotel, S.W. Broadway & Oak, Portland
The Ringside     2165 W. Burnside, Portland

# Pennsylvania

Black Angus     Rt. 272, Adamstown
Conti Cross Keys Inn     Easton Highway & Swamp Rd., Doylestown
Wooden Angel     Leopard Lane, Beaver

# Tennessee

Grisanti's     1489 Airways Blvd., Memphis

# Texas

Confederate House    4007 Westheimer, Houston
The Crow's Nest    2700 S. Hiway 75, Denison
Glasscock's    9503 Console, San Antonio
The Grape    2808 Greenbille, Dallas
Jennivine    3605 McKinney, Dallas
Joseph's    1408 Westheimer, Houston
La Cave Wine Bar    2926 N. Henderson, Dallas
The Wine Press    4217 Oak Lawn, Dallas
Woodlawn Country Club    Miller Barber Rd., Sherman

# Vermont

The Post Horn Inn    Route 11, Londonderry

# Washington

El Gaucho    624 Olive Ave., Seattle
Le Tastevin    501 Queen Anne Ave., Seattle
Rosselini's Other Place    4th & Union, Seattle

# Washington, D.C.

The American Cafe    1211 Wisconsin Ave. NW
The Carlton Wine Bar    Sheraton Carlton Hotel, 16th & K Sts. NW
Chez Maria    3338 M Street NW
Coleman's Restaurant and Wine Bar    20th & Pennsylvania Ave. NW
L'Escargot    3309 Connecticut Ave. NW
The Prime Rib    2020 K Street NW
1789 Restaurant    1226 36th St. NW

# Retail Stores

---

## Alabama

The Grapevine     2414 Canterbury Rd., Mountain Brook Village
Vine & Cheese Company     3696-B Airport Blvd., Mobile
The Vineyard     1090 U.S. 31 South, Vestavia Hills
The Wine Gallery     3720 Lorna Rd., Birmingham

## Arizona

Arcadia Wines     4513 N. Scottsdale Rd., Scottsdale
Dave's Liquors & Fine Wines     5031 N. 16th St., Phoenix
Economy Liquors     4040 N. 24th St., Phoenix
The Rum Runner     3206 E. Speedway Blvd., Tucson
Valley Fair Discount Wines & Spirits     121 E. Southern Ave., Tempe

## Arkansas

Bullard's     Cantrell at Rebsamen Park Rd., Little Rock
Foster's Liquor Store     316 Plaza Shopping Center, Blytheville

# California

A.T.C. Factory
    4505 La Jolla Village Dr., Bldg. C-10, La Jolla
    1640 Camino del Rio North, San Diego
Ace's Liquor    1104 Chapala St., Santa Barbara
Alamo Wine & Spirits    3215 Danville Blvd., Alamo
Allan's Wine & Spirits    2521 Ventura Rd., Port Hueneme
Bacchus & Assoc. Ltd.    1310 Santa Monica Blvd., Santa Monica
Beltramo's    1540 El Camino Real, Menlo Park
Bill's Foremost Liquors    2417 Sepulveda Blvd., Manhattan Beach
Bolton's    1885 Solano Ave., Berkeley
Brand X Liquor    443 S. Pacific Coast Hwy., Redondo Beach
Bottle Shop    1030 Torrey Pines Rd., La Jolla
Cabrillo Wine & Liquor    1317 S. Gaffey St., San Pedro
California Wine Merchant    3237 Pierce St., San Francisco
Cannery Gourmet    2801 Leavenworth St., San Francisco
Chalet Wines & Spirits    72-790 El Paseo, Palm Desert
Churchills Wines & Liquors    2232 Fair Oaks Blvd., Sacramento
Coit Liquors    Union & Columbus, San Francisco
Conoisseur Wine Imports    462 Bryant, San Francisco
Continental Liquor    290 Storke Rd., Goleta
The Cork and More, Inc.    South Lake Tahoe
Corti Bros.    5760 Freeport Blvd., Sacramento
Courtesy Liquor & Delicatessens
    9889 Carmel Mountain Rd., San Diego
    3963 Governor Dr., San Diego
Crane & Kelley Wine & Cheese    2111 Union St., San Francisco
Crest Liquor    3787 Ingraham, Pacific Beach
Custom Liquor House    250 John St., Salinas
Cutting Board Deli & Wines    2064 Treat Blvd., Walnut Creek
Dan's Liquors    3232 Manhattan Ave., Hermosa Beach
Del Cerro Liquor    6380 Del Cerro Blvd., San Diego
Del Mesa Liquor    6090 Friars Rd., San Diego
Delicacy Shop    1869 N. Euclid, Fullerton
Deerpark Wine & Spirits    783 Rio del Mar Blvd., Aptos
Draper & Esquin    655 Sutter St., San Francisco
Duke of Bourbon    20908 Roscoe Blvd., Canoga Park
Ernie's Wine Shop    699 St. Helena Hwy., St. Helena
Ernie's Wine Warehouse
    560 Sacramento St., San Francisco
    1492 San Mateo Ave., South San Francisco

Firehouse Wine Bar     414 Calle Principal, Monterey
Fletcher Hills Bottle Shop     2447 Fletcher Parkway, El Cajon
Foremost Wine and Spirits     6541 Westminster Ave., Westminster
Foremost-Monterey Plaza Liquors     301 Monterey Rd., South Pasadena
The Gourmet     2610 Fair Oaks Blvd., Sacramento
Gourmet Wine & Spirits     505 S. Flower St., Los Angeles
The Grape Press     410 Anaheim Hills Rd., Anaheim
Groezingers     Vintage 1870, Yountville
Hi-Time Gourmet Wine & Spirits     495 E. 17th St., Costa Mesa
Hilltop Liquor     815 Indianapolis Ave., Huntington Beach
Holiday Wine Cellar     302 West Mission, Escondido
Jackson's Wines & Spirits     Ashby & Domingo, Berkeley
Jay Vee Liquors     12191 Alcosta Blvd., San Ramon
John's     Ladera Country Shopper, Menlo Park
John Walker     111 Montgomery, San Francisco
JV     1316 University Ave., Berkeley
Kaelin's Valley Center     1435 E. Main St., El Cajon
La Crescenta Liquor     2756 Foothill, La Crescenta
La Cantina Liquors     945 Lomas Santa Fe Dr., Solana Beach
Lawry's California Center     568 San Fernando Rd., Los Angeles
The London Wine Bar     415 Sansome, San Francisco
Macy's     Stockton & O'Farrell, San Francisco
Mangrove Bottle Shop, Inc.     1348 Mangrove Ave., Chico
Marin Wine & Spirits     various locations in Marin County
Mesa Wines     200 Cliff Dr., Santa Barbara
Mickey's Holiday, Inc.     9187 Central Ave., Montclair
Midway Wine & Spirits     3040 Midway Dr., San Diego
Mill Valley Market     12 Corte Madera Ave., Mill Valley
Miratti's Fine Wines     2009 De La Vina St., Santa Barbara
Morry's of Naples     5764 E. 2nd St., Long Beach
Pap's Liquors     2604 Mendocino Ave., Santa Rosa
Patti's Deli & Gourmet     982 Gray Ave., Yuba City
Pearson's     26th & San Vicente, Los Angeles
Pierre LaFond & Co.     516 San Ysidro Rd., Montecito
Piret's     902 W. Washington St., San Diego
Rancho Bernardo Spirits Shop     12457 Rancho Bernardo Rd., San Diego
Red Carpet Liquors     1050 Howe Ave., Sacramento
Red Carpet Wine & Spirits     400 E. Glenoaks, Glendale
Richard's General Store     6501 E. Serrano Ave., Anaheim Hills
Riviera Liquor House     4114 W. Pt. Loma Blvd., San Diego
Robert's of Woodside     3015 Woodside Rd., Woodside
Sausalito Cellars     2951 Bridgeway, Sausalito
Simi Liquor     1922 Erringer Rd., Simi Valley

Sonoma Cheese Factory    2 Spain St., Sonoma
The Spirit Seller    1308 W. Olive, Porterville
Spirits of Saint Germain    3251 Holiday Court, La Jolla
Spyglass Liquors    2665 Shell Beach Rd., Shell Beach
Stanaway Bros. Food Centers, Inc.    1160 Broadway Ave., Burlingame
Temperance Liquors    197 Village Square, Stockton
Town Pump Wine & Spirit Shoppes
    11007 Chapman Ave., Garden Grove
    22505 Crenshaw Blvd., Torrance
Trader Joe's    610 S. Arroyo Park Blvd., Pasadena
Traverso's Gourmet Foods    Third & B Streets, Santa Rosa
Trumpetvine Wines    2115 Allston Way, Berkeley
Udder Corner    247 First St., Encinitas
The Uptown    7601 Greenleaf, Whittier
Valley Spirits    1045 W. Orangeburg, Modesto
Viking Liquor    1051 Edison St., Santa Ynez
The Villa    2138 4th St., San Rafael
Vintage Shoppe    434 W. Highland Ave., San Bernardino
Vineyard    1762 Garnet Ave., Pacific Beach
Wally's    10811 W. Pico Blvd., Los Angeles
Weimax Wines & Spirits    1178 Broadway Ave., Burlingame
Wine and Cheese Center    205 Jackson and 2111 Union, San Francisco
Wine Cave Liquor    2255 Cleveland Ave., Santa Rosa
The Wine House    535 Bryant St., San Francisco
The Wine Merchant    9701 Santa Monica Blvd., Beverly Hills
The Wine Merchant at the Vineyard    255 S. Palm Canyon Dr., Palm
    Springs
Wine 'n Liquor Basket    4454 Van Nuys Blvd., Sherman Oaks
The Wine Shop    2175 Chestnut St., San Francisco
Wines of California    11 Carmel Center, Carmel
Woodland Bottle Shop    2249 Grant Rd., Los Altos

# Colorado

Centennial Liquors    2721 N. 12th, Grand Junction
Century Liquor    7400 E. Hampden, Denver
El Rancho Liquors    Intersection I-70 & SH 74, Golden
Henry Hoffman's    511 18th, Denver
Heritage    7475 Arapahoe Rd., Denver
104th Ave. Liquors, Inc.    255 W. 104th Ave., Golden
Orchard Wines    5135 S. Yosemite, Denver
3-S Liquor    8021 N. Wadsworth, Denver

## Connecticut

Ashford Spirit Shoppe    Rt. 7, Box 36, Ashford
Bennie Sez Liquor Mart    1155 Post Rd., Riverside
Blum's Wines and Spirits, Inc.    110 Westfarms Mall, Farmington
Manousos Bros. Wine & Liquor    1414 Berlin Turnpike, Wethersfield
White House Liquors    178 Newington Rd., West Hartford
The Wine Merchant    49 College St., New Haven
The Wine Shop at Budget Liquor    392 Post Rd. East, Westport

## Delaware

F & N Liquor Store    2436 Faulk Rd., Wilmington
Miller Road Liquors    3062 Miller Rd., Wilmington

## Florida

ABC Liquors    Miracle Mile Plaza, Vero Beach
Causeway Wines & Spirits    1576 S.E. 3 Ct. Hillsboro Beach Blvd.,
    Deerfield Beach
Chadwick's General Store    South Seas Plantation, Captiva Island
Dean's    Governor Square, 1500 Apalachee Pkwy., Tallahassee
The Imperial Chateau Wines
    924 S. Florida Ave., Lakeland
    2500 W. Bay Dr., Largo
    2600 4th St. N., St. Petersburg
    3629 Henderson Blvd., Tampa
    2427 Aloma Ave., Winter Park
Riverside Lounge    1035 Park St., Jacksonville
Schagrins
    5979 N. Federal Hwy., Ft. Lauderdale
    1304 S.E. 17th St., Ft. Lauderdale
    3199 N. University Dr., Sunrise
Sunset Corners Package Store    8701 Sunset Dr., Miami
Wine Cask    11460 U.S. Hwy. 1, Palm Beach Gardens
The Wine & Cheese Gallery    113 N. Main St., Gainesville
Wine Kork    2516-A McMullen Booth Rd., Clearwater

## Georgia

East Side Bottle Shop    1392 Roswell Rd., Marietta
Green's Beer & Wine Store    2614 Buford Hwy., Atlanta
House of Spirits    2401 A Dawson Rd., Albany

Skinflint's    1943 Peachtree Rd. NE, Atlanta
Tower    2121 Piedmont Rd., Atlanta

# Hawaii

Village Wine Cellar    Queen & Alakea Sts., Honolulu
Vintage Wine Cellar
    Pearlridge Shopping Ctr., Lower Level, Aiea
    The Warehouse, 625 Keawe St., Honolulu
    1249 Wilder Ave., Honolulu

# Idaho

Atkinson's Market    Giacobbi Square, Ketchum
The Grapevine    123 Jefferson, Pocatello
Mussels Fish Market    3107 Overland Rd., Boise

# Illinois

Armanetti Liquors
    510 W. Lake St., Addison
    860 Lake St., Aurora
    Meadowdale Shopping Ctr., Carpentersville
    2307 N. Clark St., Chicago
    5138 W. Division St., Chicago
    5130 Fullerton Ave., Chicago
    6048 W. North Ave., Chicago
    7324 N. Western Ave., Chicago
    5425 S. Lagrange Rd., Countryside
    350 Virginia St., Crystal Lake
    7550 W. Grand Ave., Elmwood Park
    18244 S. Kedzie Ave., Hazelcrest
    1313 W. North Ave., Melrose Park
    8776 Dempster St., Niles
    4151 Dundee Rd., Northbrook
    15750 S. Harlem Ave., Orland Park
    3208 Market Plaza, Rolling Meadows
Chalet Wine & Cheese Shops
    405 W. Armitage, Chicago
    444 W. Fullerton, Chicago
    1525 E. 53rd St., Chicago
    71 Linden Ave., Glencoe
Ciota's    3018 N. Sterling, Peoria

Domino Liquors      6224 N. 2nd St., Rockford
Foremost Liquors
    740 State Line Ave., Calumet City
    2729 North Mannheim Rd., Franklin Park
    425 Townline Rd., Mundelein
    326 N. Independence Blvd., Romeoville
    6920 S. Route 83, Willowbrook
Gateway Liquor      413 W. Lincoln, Charleston
Gendler's Cellars      2518 5th Ave., Rock Island
Gold Standard Liquors
    3012 N. Broadway, Chicago
    3000 N. Clark St., Chicago
    6630 Ridge, Chicago
    153 Skokie Valley Hwy., Highland Park
    3121 Thatcher, River Grove
    5100 W. Dempster, Skokie
    1501 N. Lewis, Waukegan
Leonard Soloman's      745 N. LaSalle, Chicago
Red Arrow      6358 West Higgins, Chicago
Sam's Liquors      756 West North, Chicago
Schaefer's      9965 Grosse Point, Skokie
Sola's Liquors      14420 Indiana Ave., Riverdale
Times Square Liquors      Times Square Mall, Mount Vernon
Worldwide Liquors      6715 Northwest Hwy., Chicago

# Indiana

Albany Liquors      2511 Albany, Beech Grove
Bumble Bee Liquors      Broadway & U.S. Hwy. 12, Beverly Shores
King's Cellar      1725 N. Ironwood, South Bend
Lebamoff's Cap-N-Cork      6712 East State, Fort Wayne
Main Package Liquor      2651 S. Main St., Elkhart
Wedge's Liquors & Wines      1700 E. Broadway

# Kentucky

Shoppers Village Liquors
    316 Versailles Rd., Frankfort
    2185 Versailles Rd., Lexington
    105 E. Reynolds Rd., Lexington
    124 New Circle Rd., Lexington
    866 E. High St., Lexington
    U.S. Hwy. 60, Winchester

# Louisiana

The Compleat Wine Cellar & Bottle Shop     3410 Jackson, Alexandria
Liquor Mart     3106 Youree St., Shreveport
Martin's Wine Cellar     3827 Baronne St., New Orleans
Spirits Inc.     4488 Florida Blvd., Baton Rouge
The Vintner     501 Metairie Rd., Metairie

# Maine

Auburn Wine & Cheese Shed     563 Center St., Auburn

# Maryland

Camelot Wines & Liquors     300 Washington Blvd., Laurel
Cran Brook Liquors, Inc.     588 Cran Brook Rd., Cockeysville
Mills Liquors     87 Main St., Annapolis
Perring Wine & Spirits     1987 Joppa Rd., Baltimore
Rosen's Liquors, Inc.     5411 York Rd., Baltimore
State Line Liquors, Inc.     Route 279 & Iron Hill Rd., Elkton

# Massachusetts

Andover Liquors     209 N. Main St., Andover
Berman's     55 Massachusetts Ave., Lexington
Blanchard's, Inc.
    103 Harvard Ave., Allston
    675 Washington St., Newtonville
Burns Discount Liquors     1908 Wilbraham Rd., Springfield
Harvard Wine & Liquor     288 Harvard St., Brookline
Lavin's Wine, Liquor & Cheese     330 Old Connecticut Path, Wayland
Warehouse Wine Cellar     51 Union St., Worcester
Wine Cellars of Silene     320 Bear Hill Rd., Waltham
The Wine Company Ltd.     35 Whiting St., Hingham
Wine Specialties Inc.     423 Washington St., Stoughton

# Michigan

Alban's Bottle & Basket Shoppe     188 N. Hunter, Birmingham
Bacchus Wines & Spirits     3112 Oakland Drive, Kalamazoo
The Blue Goat     875 E. Front St., Traverse City
Cesaron's Wine Rack     6476 Orchard Lake Road, West Bloomfield
Clover Wine Cellar     10988 Allen Rd., Taylor

Cloverleaf Market     28905 Telegraph, Southfield
The Corkscrew     3538 Beecher, Flint
G.B. Russo & Sons Ltd.     2770 29th St., Grand Rapids
Gibbs Worldwide Wines     9999 Gratiot, Detroit
Goodrich's Spartan Shop     940 Trowbridge Rd., East Lansing
Hoyt's Wine & Spirits     543 South Main, Lapeer
Lambrecht's Liquors     2926 Niles Ave., St. Joseph's
Merchant of Vino     4050 Rochester, Troy
Mr. Mack's Partyville & Wine Shoppe     927 Inkster Rd., Garden City
The Red Wagon Wine Shoppe
     1571 N. Main, Clawson
     2940 S. Rochester Rd., Rochester
Russo's     2770 29th St. S.E., Grand Rapids
The Ren Cellar     Detroit Plaza Hotel, Renaissance Center, Detroit
Showerman's IGA     111 South LaFayette, South Lyon
Village Corner     601 S. Forest, Ann Arbor

## Minnesota

Andy's Crossroads Liquor     1201 S. Broadway, Rochester
Byerly's Wines and Spirits
     5719 Duluth St., Golden Valley
     3777 Park Center Blvd., St. Louis Park
Surdyk's Liquor     303 E. Hennepin Ave., Minneapolis

## Mississippi

Frontage Road Package Store     4760 Interstate 55 North, Jackson

## Missouri

The Deli     2318 N. Belt, St. Joseph
Happy Hollow Liquor Stores
     1801 Westport Rd., Kansas City
     1606 W. 75th St., Kansas City
     400 W. 103rd St., Kansas City

## Montana

Casey's Pharmacy Wine Corner     111 N. Last Chance Gulch, Helena
Wholesale Wine Merchant     6620 Pinewood Lane, Missoula

# Nebraska

Bottles Unlimited     3218 West College, Grand Island
Cliff's     1200 O Street, Lincoln


# Nevada

Ben's Discount Liquor
     901 W. Fourth St., Reno
     190 S. Center St., Reno
The Corkscrew     238 S. Arlington Ave., Reno


# New Jersey

Borough Cordial Shop     363 Bloomfield Ave., Caldwell
Burke's Package Store     6 Sparta Ave., Sparta
Caruso's Wines Ltd.     1120 S. Avenue, W., Westfield
Colonial Spirit Shoppe     611 Park Ave., Freehold
Eatontown Wines & Liquors     66 Hwy. 26, Eatontown
Fine Wines & Spirits     14 Riveredge Rd., Tenafly
Food Town Liquors     99 Ridgedale Ave., Cedar Knolls
Freddy's Liquor     570 W. Cuthbert Rd., Haddon Township
Hamilton Wine and Liquors     2321 Route 22, Union
Ho Ho Kus Wines     626 N. Maple Ave., Ho Ho Kus
Home Liquors     501 Schuyler Ave., Lyndhurst
Joseph's Liquor Store     1525 N. High St., Millville
Nutley Wine Shop     559 Franklin Ave., Nutley
Plainsboro Package Store, Inc.     4 Schalks Crossing, Plainsboro
Seplow Liquors     5 Woodside Ave., Newton
Smith's Liquors     Junction #9 & Elton-Adelphia Rd., Freehold
State Prize Liquors     2191 Morris Ave., Union
V.G. Liquors-Lawnside Liquor Mart     116 N. Whitehorse Pike,
     Lawnside
Village Wine & Liquors     Route 24, Mendham
Welsh's Fine Wines and Spirits     8 S. Union St., Lambertville
The Wine Cellar     Branch Pike at Rt. 130, Cinnaminson
The Wine Rack     Sutton Park Shopping Ctr., Flanders
Woodbridge Center Liquors     301 Woodbridge Center Dr., Woodbridge
Wyckoff Wine & Spirits     Corner Clinton & Wyckoff Aves., Wyckoff

# New York

Acker, Merrall & Condit     2373 Broadway, New York
Ardsley Wine & Liquors     976 Lexington Ave., New York
Around World Liquors     Old Little Britain Rd., Newburgh
Barbara's World of Wine     197 Wolf Rd., Albany
Barton's Liquors     511 Conklin St., Farmingdale
Bay Ridge Liquor Co., Inc.     425 86th St., Brooklyn
Bremer & Bullock Liquors     1314 Oneida St., Utica
Browncroft Liquors     268 Winston Rd. North, Rochester
Carload Liquors     TSS Mall, Route 110, Melville
Century Liquors     630 Ridge Road, W., Rochester
Columbus Cicle Liquors     1780 Broadway, New York
Cork & Bottle Ltd.     First Ave. & East 63rd St., New York
Country Liquor Supermarkets
     Routes 9 & 236, Guideboard Rd., Halfmoon
     R.D. #11, Clifton Park
Crazy Billy's Deer Park Liquors     1887 Deer Park Ave., Deer Park
Crossroads     53 West 14th St., New York
Currier's Wine & Spirits     2256 Hudson Ave., Rochester
Dom & Carl Wine & Liquor     201 Thompson St., New York
Drive Spirits     2903 Broadway, New York
East Hill Liquors     Cayuga Mall, Triphammer Rd., Ithaca
Edras Liquors, Inc.     533 Boston Post Rd., Port Chester
Esposito Wines & Liquors, Inc.     608 West 207th St., New York
Excelsior Wines & Liquors     332 West 57th St., New York
First Avenue Wine & Spirits     383 First Ave., New York
Forest Hills Liquor     10809 Queens Blvd., Forest Hills
Gilbert Wines & Liquors     1161 Merrick Ave., North Merrick
Giuliano's Liquor City     Bruckner Blvd. & White Plains Rd., Bronx
Gold Star Wines & Liquors     103-05 Queens Blvd., Forest Hills
Good Spirits Wines & Liquor     480 New Rochelle Rd., Bronxville
Gotham Liquors     1543 Third Ave., New York
Grand Wine & Liquor     30-05 31st St., Astoria
Grape & Grain Wines & Liquors     321 Amsterdam Ave., New York
Great Eastern Liquor Store     600 Hempstead Turnpike, Elmont
Green Hill Liquors     6003 S. Salina St., Syracuse
Greenvale Liquors, Inc.     80 Northern Blvd., Greenvale
Henner's International Wine Room     544-554 Chili Ave., Rochester
High Hopes Wine & Liquor Corp.     1755 Crosby Ave., Bronx
Hillside World Wide Liquors     740 Franklin Ave., Franklin Square
Hodge Liquor     463 Elmwood Ave., Buffalo
Hoffend Liquor Store     657-59 Pittsford Victor Rd., Pittsford

House of Bacchus     1050 Ridge Road E., Rochester
International Wine Gallery     270 Nassau Blvd., Garden City South
Jacoves Liquor Store     20 Hempstead Turnpike, West Hempstead
Kings Liquor Plaza     24-81 Flatbush Ave., Brooklyn
Leroy Package Store, Inc.     64 Leroy St., Binghamton
Liquor City of Majors     2239 Forest Ave., Staten Island
Liquor Giant     Staten Island Mall, Staten Island
Liquor Square     3020 Erie Blvd. East, Syracuse
MAB Liquors     1552 Front St., East Meadow
Manhattan Chateau     1122 Third Ave., New York
Manley's Wine & Spirits     35 Eighth Ave., New York
Master Wine & Liquor     Saw Mill River Rd., Elmsford
Maxwell's Wines & Spirits     1657 First Ave., New York
Miron Liquor & Wine     9 W & Boice Lane, Kingston
Morrell & Co.     307 East 53rd St., New York
North End Liquors     2509 Webster Ave., Bronx
Northside Liquors     Ithaca Plaza, Elmira Rd., Ithaca
Okst Wine & Liquor     1610 Main St., Port Jefferson
Orange Plaza     Route 211, East Middletown
Park Avenue Liquor Shop     292 Madison Ave., New York
Pascale Liquors     7621 Oswego Rd., Liverpool
Path Liquors, Inc.     306 Middle Country Rd., Coram
Peninsula Wine & Liquor     1326 Peninsula Blvd., Hewlett
Pop's Wine & Liquor     256 Long Beach Rd., Island Park
Post Wines & Liquors     536 Jericho Turnpike, Syosset
Queens Wine & Liquors     59-03 71st Ave., Ridgewood
Richmond Liquor Corp.     Staten Island Mall, Staten Island
Ritter Wine & Liquor     549 Classon Ave., Brooklyn
Seaholm Wines & Liquors     198 New York Ave., Huntington
Sherry-Lehmann, Inc.     679 Madison Ave., New York
Shoppers Paradise     24-38 Central Ave., Spring Valley
67 Liquors     68th St. & Columbus Ave., New York
Southeast Wine & Liquor     Southeast Plaza, Route 22, Brewster
Spirits Cellar     2199 E. Henrietta Rd., Rochester
Steward Spirits Shop     76-78 Covert Ave., Stewart Manor
Supermarket Liquors     290 W. Sunrise Hwy., Valley Stream
Sutton Wine Shop     403 East 57th St., New York
Thriftway Liquors, Inc.     689 Hillside Ave., New Hyde Park
Thruway Liquors     420-A Thruway Mall, Harlem & Walden Aves.,
     Cheektowaga
Tops Liquors     2816 Avenue U, Brooklyn
Van Deusen Warehouse     70 W. Merrick Rd., Freeport
Vanderbilt Wine & Liquors     26 Vanderbilt Motor Parkway, Commack

Villa Liquors    2461 Jericho Turnpike, Garden City Park
The Village Wine & Spirit Shop    486 A Sixth Ave., New York
Webster Central Liquors    980 Ridge Rd., Webster
The Wine Cellar    2108-R Northern Blvd., Manhasset
The Wine Merchants    108-09 Queens Blvd., Forest Hills
Wine Shop    3025 Main St., Amherst
Winetasters of Westchester    100 Chatsworth Ave., Larchmont
Yonkers Liquor Masters    2350 Central Park Ave., Yonkers
Young's Liquors    505 Plandome Rd., Manhasset
Zachy's    20 E. Parkway, Scarsdale
Zanetti's    605 Old Country Rd., Westbury

## North Carolina

A Cut Above    3500 West Polo Rd., Winston-Salem
Ale and Artifacts Ltd.    5940 South Blvd., Charlotte
Belk-Tyler Co.    Carolina East Mall, Greenville
Buena Vista Wine & Cheese    1703 Robinhood Rd., Winston–Salem
Kathryn's Cheese House/Weinhaus    86 Patton Ave., Ashville
The Landing Wine & Cheese Shop    53 D Causeway Dr., Wrightsville

## North Dakota

Happy Harry's Bottle Shop    2215 Gateway Dr., Grand Forks
Polar Liquors    306 Business Loop West, Jamestown
Polar Package Place    19th Ave. & N. University Dr., Fargo

## Ohio

Arrow Wine Stores
    72950 Far Hills Ave., Dayton
    1072 Patterson Rd., Dayton
    Route 725 at McEwan Rd., Dayton
Cellini's Wine Cellar    19300 Detroit Road, Rocky River
Gentiles, The Wine Sellers
    6072 Busch Blvd., Columbus
    1565 King Ave., Columbus
The Luxembourg House    7789 Cooper Rd., Montgomery
Olympia Beverage Center    502 Lewis Ave., Toledo
Pat O'Brien's Ave. Beverage    Mentor
Pogue's 4th Street Market & Wine Bar    Cincinnati
Rozi's Wine House, Inc.    14900 Detroit Ave., Lakewood
Sam B's    Wooster & State St., Bowling Green

Shaker Square Beverage   30800 Pinetree Rd., Pepper Pike
Tarpy's Beverages and Delicatessen
    1805 Kingsdale Center, Columbus
    1924 Brice Rd., Reynoldsburg
Warzy's Deli and Wine Shops
    1068 North Main St., Bowling Green
    3400 Glendale Ave., Toledo
West Point Market   1711 W. Market St., Akron
The Wine Merchant
    I-270 & N. High St., Columbus
    437 E. Sandusky, Findlay
Wines, Inc.   915 E. Dublin-Granville Rd., Columbus

# Oklahoma

Ranch Acres Liquor   3324 A East 31st, Tulsa

# Oregon

Of Grape & Grain
    49 West 29th Ave., Eugene
    160 Oakway Rd., Eugene
Pepi's Wine Shop   3055 S.W. Cedar Hills, Beaverton
Strohecker's   2855 S.W. Patton Road, Portland

## South Carolina

The Wine Shoppe   14 Greenwood Dr., Hilton Head Island
Wine World   106 Georgia Ave., North Augusta

## Tennessee

Buster's Poplar & Highland Liquors   3493 Poplar Ave., Memphis
Mendenhall Square Liquor Store   5382 Mendenhall Mall, Memphis

## Texas

A.J.'s Discount Liquors & Wines   3120 Calder, Beaumont
Bee Gee's   718 S. Clark, Abilene
Cecil's Liquor Store   Hwy. 87 South, Lubbock
Doc's Liquor Stores
    2400 Canyon Dr., Amarillo
    4312 W. 45th St., Amarillo

Driggs No. 3      3000 S. Woodlawn, Denison
Feldman's Valley Wide, Inc.      116 W. Van Buren St., Harlingen
Jef's Wine Cellar      FM 2483 & FM 2271, Morgan's Point
K & P Liquor Store      5026 Highway 75 South, Denison
Kaleidoscope      4200 S. Alameda, Corpus Christi
Mark's Liquor Store      Hwy. 87 South, Lubbock
Marty's      3316 Oak Lawn, Dallas
North Texas Liquors      3109 Woodlawn, Denison
Pen Foods      8101 Callaghan Rd., San Antonio
Rebel Liquors      14072 Memorial Dr., Houston
Reubin's Bottle Shop      8311 Research St., Austin
Richard's
    6532 San Felipe, Houston
    5630 Richmond, Houston
    2411 S. Gessner, Houston
Sigel Liquors      2960 Anode St., Dallas
Spec's      2410 Smith, Houston
Texas Stores, Inc.      8442 Gault Lane, San Antonio
The Well      2408 N. Big Spring, Midland

## Virginia

Bacchus & Beer      6003 W. Broad St., Richmond
The Cheese Shoppe      424 Prince George St., Williamsburg
Cheese Villa      9575 Braddock Rd., Fairfax
Chez Andre      5905 High Street W., Portsmouth
The Compleat Wine Cellar & Bottle Shop      3410 Jackson St.,
    Alexandria
The Gourmet Warehouse      815 King St., Alexandria
Taste Unlimited Inc.
    635 Hilltop West, Virginia Beach
    1619 Colley St., Norfolk
The Warwick Cheese Shoppe Inc.      10850 Warwick Blvd.,
    Newport News

## Washington

Champion Cellars      108 Denny Way, Seattle
La Cantina      University Village Shopping Center, Seattle
Pike & Western Wine Merchants      Pike Place Market, Seattle
The Wine & Cheese Merchants      James Center, 6905 D West 19, Tacoma

# Washington, D.C.

Bell Wine Shop    1821 M St. NW, Washington
Calvert Wine Shop    2312 Wisconsin Ave. NW, Washington
Capitol Hill Wine & Cheese    611 Pennsylvania Ave. SE, Washington
Harry's Liquor, Wine & Cheese Shoppe    401 M St. SW, Washington
Morris Miller Liquors    7804 Alaska Ave. NW, Washington

# Wisconsin

Badger Liquor Shop    402 State St., Madison
Bradley Liquor Inc.    4365 W. BradleyRd., Milwaukee
Mid City Liquors    510 N. Oneida St., Appleton
The Wine Cask    4600 W. Brown Deer Rd., Milwaukee

# Wyoming

Marc VII — Copper Corner Inc.    867 N. 3rd St., Laramie

# NOTES

# NOTES

NOTES

**NOTES**